D1081105

Pocket
SEOUL
TOP SIGHTS • LOCAL LIFE • MADE EASY

Trent Holden

In This Book

QuickStart Guide

Your keys to understanding the city – we help you decide what to do and how to do it

Need to Know
Tips for a smooth trip

Neighbourhoods
What's where

Explore Seoul

The best things to see and do, neighbourhood by neighbourhood

Top Sights
Make the most of your visit

Local Life
The insider's city

The Best of Seoul

The city's highlights in handy lists to help you plan

Best Walks
See the city on foot

Seoul's Best...
The best experiences

Survival Guide

Tips and tricks for a seamless, hassle-free city experience

Getting Around
Travel like a local

Essential Information
Including where to stay

Our selection of the city's best places to eat, drink and experience:

◉ **Sights**

❌ **Eating**

🍷 **Drinking**

⭐ **Entertainment**

🔒 **Shopping**

These symbols give you the vital information for each listing:

☑ Telephone Numbers
🕐 Opening Hours
P Parking
🚭 Nonsmoking
@ Internet Access
📶 Wi-Fi Access
🥗 Vegetarian Selection
📖 English-Language Menu

🚸 Family-Friendly
🐾 Pet-Friendly
🚌 Bus
⛴ Ferry
Ⓜ Metro
Ⓢ Subway
🚊 Tram
🚆 Train

Find each listing quickly on maps for each neighbourhood:

Bar Hemingway

16 🍷 Map p233, B2

Legend has it that Hemi self, wielding a machine rate this timber-pan tered bar during showpiece is a en by Papa ar town. Dress s.com; Hôtel Rit 🕐6.30pm-2a

6 ◉ *Plac*

Lonely Planet's Seoul

Lonely Planet Pocket Guides are designed to get you straight to the heart of the city.

Inside you'll find all the must-see sights, plus tips to make your visit to each one really memorable. We've split the city into easy-to-navigate neighbourhoods and provided clear maps so you'll find your way around with ease. Our expert authors have searched out the best of the city: walks, food, nightlife and shopping, to name a few. Because you want to explore, our 'Local Life' pages will take you to some of the most exciting areas to experience the real Seoul.

And of course you'll find all the practical tips you need for a smooth trip: itineraries for short visits, how to get around, and how much to tip the guy who serves you a drink at the end of a long day's exploration.

It's your guarantee of a really great experience.

Our Promise

You can trust our travel information because Lonely Planet authors visit the places we write about, each and every edition. We never accept freebies for positive coverage, so you can rely on us to tell it like it is.

QuickStart Guide

Welcome to Seoul

Overcoming the upheavals of war, cultural destruction, dictatorships and economic ruin, Seoul has not only landed on its feet, but emerged as one of the world's great 21st-century cities. A fascinating mix of old and new, Seoul balances traditional culture with contemporary attractions. With amazing food, happening nightlife and a lively arts scene, Seoul's enjoying a renaissance not to be missed.

Lantern festival, Cheong-gye-cheon (p34)
GLENN SUNDEEN · TIGERPAL/GETTY IMAGES ©

Seoul
Top Sights

Changdeokgung (p26)

The World Heritage–listed Changdeokgung was built in the early 15th century as a secondary palace to Gyeongbokgung. The most charming section is Huwon, a 'secret garden' that is a royal horticultural idyll.

Gyeongbokgung
(p24)

Admire the scale and artistry of Gyeong-bokgung, the largest of Seoul's palaces. It's fronted by the grand gateway Gwanghwa-mun, where you can watch the changing of the guard.

Jogye-sa (p28)

Learn about Buddhism at Jogye-sa, one of Seoul's most active temples and the epi-centre of the spectacular Lotus Lantern Festival in May.

The DMZ (p96)

The 250km-long and 4km-wide Demilitarized Zone (DMZ) is the heavily mined and guarded border that separates North Korea from South Korea. An entrenched symbol of the Cold War, the border has become a surreal tourist draw.

Deoksugung (p50)

Enjoy the changing of the guard outside Deoksugung before heading inside to wander the pleasant palace grounds. Architectural fans will be intrigued by its mix of Joseon-era buildings and neoclassical 20th-century designs.

National Museum of Korea (p82)

Survey centuries of Korean culture and art at the mammoth National Museum of Korea and take time to explore the attached gardens.

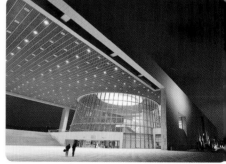

Namsan & N Seoul Tower (p46)

Protected within a 109-hectare park and crowned by N Seoul Tower one of Seoul's most distinctive architectural features, Namsan is the most central of the city's four guardian mountains.

Dongdaemun Design Plaza (p116)

Rising up behind the lively shopping district is the sleek, silvery form of the Zaha Hadid–designed DDP. An architectural show-stopper that could hardly be more 21st century in its conception, the DDP has affirmed itself as one of Seoul's most striking landmarks.

Namdaemun Market (p48)

Join the masses and head into Namdaemun Market to take in its pulsating energy. At Korea's largest market, you'll eat very well and snare plenty of bargains.

Olympic Park (p112)

A centrepiece for the 1988 Olympics, and still the site of many of its stadiums, this giant park mixes large tracts of nature with 700-year-old fortifications, museums and 200 quirky sculptures.

Seoul
Local Life

Insider tips to help you find the real city

Amid visiting its palaces and museums, leave time to enjoy the things locals most love about their city. From sipping tea in a wooden *hanok* (traditional wooden house) and getting merry with *makgeolli* (milky rice wine) to indulging in extravagances south of the river, local experiences, for many travellers, are the highlight of a visit to Seoul.

Hipster Hongdae (p66)

▶ Food and drink
▶ Live music and clubs

Seoul doesn't get much cooler than the student neighbourhood of Hongdae in the city's west. It's a great place for hanging out or moseying around vintage stores, cool cafes, bars, galleries and indie markets. Nightlife is also a highlight: there are plenty of great band venues or clubs with tops DJs.

Northern Seoul (p42)

▶ Urban art
▶ Nature

The neighborhoods in Seoul's northern confines are prime areas for visitors seeking local experiences, particularly those with a love of the arts. Here you'll visit vibrant alleyways full of colourful murals, quirky private museums and galleries, and many theatres hosting performance art.

Oppa Gangnam Style (p100)

▶ Shopping
▶ K-Pop

Among the cosmetic surgery clinics and Chihuahua-clutching fashionistas, upscale Apgujeong Rodeo St lies at the heart of Gangnam's lavishness and excesses. This walk offers a fascinating insight to see how the other half live, with luxury shopping, chic galleries and K-Pop sights along the way.

Bar-Hopping in HBC (p84)

▶ Craft beer
▶ Traditional Korean alcohol

There's definitely no shortage of spots to carouse at in Itaewon, from seedy bars to chic clubs. For a more local experience, head to Haebangchon (HBC), a once downtrodden and gritty neighbourhood that's reinvented itself as one of Itaewon's coolest areas. This evening out takes you to its best craft-brew pubs, cocktail bars and cherished locals.

Korean barbecue and side dishes (p90)

Pop musician, Hongdae (p64)

SIMON RICHMOND/GETTY IMAGES ©

Exploring Bukchon Hanok Village (p30)

▶ Hanok
▶ Teahouses

In contrast to Seoul's rapid-fire modernisation and high-rises, the charming backstreets of Bukchon offer a glimpse into its past. The neighbourhood is famous for its atmospheric *hanok* (traditional wooden houses), and as you stroll through, you'll find many have been converted into teahouses, museums, bars and even pizzerias.

Other great places to experience the city like a local:

Koong (p38)

Story of the Blue Star (p40)

Noryangjin Fish Market (p73)

Seoul Forest (p121)

Seoul Yangnyeongsi Herb Medicine Market (p125)

Jungang Market (p124)

Neurin Maeul (p108)

HBC Gogitjip (p91)

Jamsil Baseball Stadium (p110)

Mullae Arts Village (p70)

Seoul
Day Planner

Day One

Start your tour of **Gyeongbok-gung** (p24) at the palace's expertly restored main gate, Gwanghwamun, where you can watch the pageantry of the changing of the guard on the hour. Explore the winding streets of **Bukchon Hanok Village** (p30) and Insa-dong, pausing for refreshments at a cafe or teahouse in between browsing the equally ubiquitous art galleries and craft stores. For lunch dine cheaply at **Tobang** (p29) or in style at **Min's Club** (p130).

Join the afternoon tour of **Changdeokgung** (p26), which also includes the Huwon (Secret Garden). Explore the wooded grounds of the venerable **Jongmyo** (p34) shrine, which houses the spirit tablets of the Joseon kings and queens. For dinner sample Korean street food at **Gwangjang Market** (p122).

Head to Myeongdong and take your seat at a fun nonverbal show such as **Nanta** (p61). Be dazzled by the bright lights and retail overload of **Myeong-dong** (p44) and neighbouring **Namdaemun Market** (p48), where the stalls stay open all night.

Day Two

Survey centuries of Korean history and art by dipping into the vast collection of the **National Museum of Korea** (p82). Shuttle over to the west side of Yongsan-gu to enjoy the contemporary art and architecture at the splendid **Leeum Samsung Museum of Art** (p88).

Tuck into authentic barbecue from the American South at **Linus' BBQ** (p89) and browse some of Itaewon's boutiques then, for a postlunch workout, hike up **Namsan** to **N Seoul Tower** (p46). It's not a difficult climb, but if you don't have the energy there's a cable car or a bus. It's very romantic watching the sun set from atop this central mountain as the night lights of Seoul flicker into life. On the slopes of Namsan you can savour delicious bibimbap at **Mokmyeoksanbang** (p58).

Freshen up with a steam in the saunas and a soak in the tubs at the **Dragon Hill Spa & Resort** (p88). Return to **Itaewon** (p80) for dinner and a fun night of hopping between cafes, bars and dance clubs.

Short on time?
We've arranged Seoul's must-sees into these day-by-day itineraries to make sure you see the very best of the city in the time you have available.

Day Three

Avoid the crowds by heading up the slopes of Naksan early to admire street art and murals at **Ihwa Maeul** (p43). Take advantage of sweeping views with breakfast and coffee at **On the Hill Cafe** (p43). For even better views continue further up to Naksan Park, which features sections of the original **Seoul Wall** (p47). Upon your descent pop in for a look at the eccentric **Lock Museum** (p43), with its quirky collection.

On flat ground again, stock up on for a picnic lunch and jump on the subway to **Seoul Forest** (p121). Hire a bicycle for a leisurely pedal among the green spaces in the heart of the city. Spend the afternoon browsing through fascinating collectibles at the lively **Seoul Folk Flea Market** (p124), then head to Dongdaemun for a history lesson at **Seoul City Wall Museum** (p119). Put it all into context at **Heunginjimun** (p119).

Admire the 21st-century architectural styling of **Dongdaemun Design Plaza** (p116). A short walk from here will lead you to the photogenic **Gwangjang Market** (p122), famous for its delicious mungbean pancakes. Backtrack to **Dongdaemun Market** (p124), when at night it takes on a different persona, awakening in a shopping frenzy.

Day Four

Both contemporary art and panoramic views up and down the Han can be enjoyed at **63 Sky Art Gallery** (p72) on Yeouido. Hire a bicycle in Hangang Riverside Park and pedal out to **Seonyudo Park** (p72) on an island in the Han River. Pick your own seafood and have it cooked at **Noryangjin Fish Market** (p73).

If you're interested in contemporary architecture, then **Ewha Womans University's** (p70) stunning entrance building and **KT&G Sangsang-Madang** (p67) in Hongdae are both worth seeing. Hongdae and neighbouring Sangsu-dong and Yeonnam-dong are brimming with hipster hang-outs; if it's Saturday you can shop for quirky, original craft souvenirs at the **Free Market** (p78) or **Dongjin Market** (p78).

A late-afternoon visit to the atmospheric Buddhist temple **Bongeun-sa** (p103) can segue nicely into browsing the boutiques along Apgujeong, such as **10 Corso Como Seoul** (p110). After treating yourself to neo-Korean cuisine at **Jungsik** (p107) for dinner pitch up at the **Some Sevit** (p103) by 9pm to see the day's last floodlit flourish of the **Moonlight Rainbow Fountain** (p103) off the Banpo Bridge.

Need to Know

**For more information,
see Survival Guide (p153)**

Currency
Korean won (₩)

Language
Korean

Visas
Australian, UK, US and most Western
European citizens receive a 90-day entry
permit on arrival.

Money
ATMs widely available. Credit cards
accepted by most businesses, but some
smaller food places and markets are cash
only.

Mobile Phones
South Korea uses the CDMA digital
standard; check compatibility with your
phone provider. Phones can be hired at the
airport and elsewhere.

Time
GMT/UTC plus nine hours. No daylight
saving.

Plugs & Adaptors
Electrical current is 220V standard at 60Hz;
two round pins with no earth.

Tipping
Not a Korean custom, and is not expected.

❶ Before You Go

Your Daily Budget

Budget less than ₩100,000
▶ Dorm bed ₩20,000
▶ Street food ₩1000–₩5000
▶ Hiking up Namsan: free
▶ Entry to National Museum of Korea: free

Midrange ₩100,000–₩300,000
▶ *Hanok* (traditional guesthouse) ₩70,000
▶ *Galbi* (barbecued meat) meal ₩50,000
▶ Theatre ticket ₩40,000

Top End more than ₩300,000
▶ Hotel ₩200,000
▶ Royal Korean banquet ₩70,000
▶ DMZ tour ₩100,000

Useful Websites

Visit Seoul (www.visitseoul.net) The official
government site to everything about the city.

Seoul (http://magazine.seoulselection.com)
Online version of monthly magazine with its
finger on the city's pulse.

Lonely Planet (www.lonelyplanet.com/seoul)
Destination information, hotel bookings,
traveller forum and more.

Advance Planning

Two months before Book flights and accommodation; start learning *hangeul* (the Korean
alphabet) and train for hiking up mountains.
If visiting April to June, book for Moonlight
Tours of Changdeokgung.

Three weeks before Plan itinerary; book
DMZ tour and Templestay program.

One week before Make reservations at
top-end restaurants; buy concert tickets.

2 Arriving in Seoul

The main international gateway is **Incheon International Airport** (📞02-1577 2600; www.airport.kr; 📶), 52km west of central Seoul on the island of Yeongjongdo. A handful of international flights also arrive at **Gimpo International Airport** (📞02-1661 2626; gimpo.airport.co.kr; West Seoul), 18km west of the city centre.

✈ From Incheon International Airport

A'REX express trains travel to Seoul station ₩8000 (43 minutes), as do commuter trains ₩4150 (53 minutes), which also stop at Hongik University for those staying in Hongdae. From Seoul station transfer to your destination via Seoul's efficient subway system. A bus to city-centre hotels is ₩10,000 (one hour); a taxi around ₩65,000.

✈ From Gimpo International Airport

A'REX trains run to Seoul station (₩1450, 15 minutes) or you can take the subway (₩1250, 35 minutes). Both bus (₩7500) and taxi (around ₩35,000) will be slower – around 40 minutes to an hour, depending on traffic.

🚆 Seoul Station

Long-distance trains arrive at the centrally located **Seoul station** (S Line 1 or 4 to Seoul station). It's the the hub of the domestic rail network operated by **Korean National Railroad** (www.letskorail.com). Lines 1 and 4 connect Seoul station with the city, while city buses and taxis depart from the east side of the station.

3 Getting Around

Buy a T-Money card (₩3000; http://eng. t-money.co.kr), which provides a ₩100 discount per trip on bus, subway, taxi and train fares. Subway is by the best way of getting around, with an efficient, speedy and cheap service that links the entire city. Taxis are also reasonably priced and good for short trips.

S Subway

The **subway** (www.smrt.co.kr) is the best way to get around with its extensive network, frequent services and inexpensive fares.

🚗 Taxi

Best for short trips; basic fare starts at ₩3000 for the first 2km.

🚌 Bus

The **bus system** (www.bus.go.kr; ⏱5.30am-midnight) is handy for routes around Namsan; less so for other places.

🚲 Bicycle

Hire for pedalling along the Han River and through Olympic Park.

🚗 Car Hire

Useful only for long trips out of the city; expect to pay from ₩80,000 per day.

Seoul
Neighbourhoods

Gyeongbokgung ◉

Jogye-sa ◉

Hongdae & Around (p64)
A creative hub populated by students, artists and indie musicians. A cool, arty vibe, plus plenty of boutiques and bars.

Deoksugung ◉

Namdaemun ◉ Market

Namsan & N Seoul Tower

National Museum of Korea ◉

Itaewon & Around (p80)
Popular with the expat community, Itaewon has a heap of cool sights, bars and restaurants.

◉ **Top Sights**
National Museum of Korea

Worth a Trip
◉ **Top Sights**
Olympic Park
The Demilitarized Zone (DMZ) & Joint Security Area (JSA)

Gwanghwamun & Around (p22)

Home to many of Seoul's most famous sights, including World Heritage–listed palaces and temples.

⊙ Top Sights

Gyeongbokgung

Changdeokgung

Jogye-sa

> Changdeokgung

Dongdaemun
⊙ *Design Plaza*

Dongdaemun & Eastern Seoul (p114)

Markets and late-night shopping combined with excellent history, contemporary sights and local experiences.

⊙ Top Sights

Dongdaemun Design Plaza

Myeong-dong & Jung-gu (p44)

This downtown district has outstanding sightseeing, theatre and shopping opportunities.

⊙ Top Sights

Namsan & N Seoul Tower

Namdaemun Market

Deoksugung

Gangnam & Apgujeong (p98)

Famous for its residents' over-the-top luxurious lifestyles, this affluent area also has great sights and eating, and an entertainment zone.

Explore
Seoul

Worth a Trip

Namdaemun Market (p48)
MANFRED GOTTSCHALK/GETTY IMAGES ©

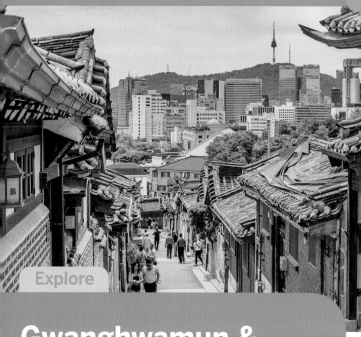

Explore

Gwanghwamun & Around

The centuries-old heart of Seoul revolves around these once-regal palace quarters. Between Gyeongbokgung and Changdeokgung, Bukchon covers several smaller areas famous for its traditional *hanok* wooden homes. West of Gyeongbokgung, Seochon is popular for strolling between galleries, cafes and boutiques. South of Bukchon are the mazelike and touristy streets of Insa-dong, and the *hanok* area of Ikseon-dong.

The Sights in a Day

☼ Begin the day at **Gyeongbok-gung** (p24) to watch the hourly ceremonial changing of the guard before exploring its palace grounds. Then go wandering among the winding streets of Insa-dong and **Bukcheon Hanok Village** (p30; pictured left), pausing for a cuppa at traditional *hanok* teahouses and to shop for quality souvenirs at art galleries and craft stores.

☼ Join the afternoon tour of **Changdeokgung** (p26), which also includes the Huwon (Secret Garden). Explore the wooded grounds of the venerable shrine **Jongmyo** (p34), housing the spirit tablets of the Joseon kings and queens.

☾ Go for an afternoon tipple at a refurbished *hanok* turned chic bar at **Sik Mool** (p40), and then sample Korean craft beers at **Brew 3.14** (p40). You can eat at either of these places, or treat yourself to a classy night out with dinner at **GastroTong** (p40) followed by a show at **Sejong Center for the Performing Arts** (p41).

For a local's day in Bukchon Hanok Village, see p30.

◉ Top Sights

Gyeongbokgung (p24)

Changdeokgung (p26)

Jogye-sa (p28)

◯ Local Life

Exploring Bukchon Hanok Village (p30)

♥ Best of Seoul

Eating

Tongin Market Box Lunch Cafe (p38)

Congdu (p38)

Balwoo Gongyang (p39)

GastroTong (p40)

Drinking

Sik Mool (p40)

Dawon (p40)

Brew 3.14 (p40)

Shopping

KCDF Gallery (p41)

Insa-dong Maru (p41)

Getting There

 Subway Line 1, 3 or 5; Anguk subway is best for Insa-dong and Bukchon.

Top Sights
Gyeongbokgung

Originally built in 1395, Gyeongbokgung (Palace of Shining Happiness) served as the principal royal residence until it was burnt down by the invading Japanese in 1592. Rebuilt 300 years later, the palace consisted of 330 buildings and had up to 3000 staff, including 140 eunuchs, all serving the royal family. During Japanese colonial rule in the 20th century, most of the palace was again destroyed – much of what you see today are accurate recent reconstructions.

경복궁

◉ Map p32, C2

www.royalpalace.go.kr/html/eng

adult/child ₩3000/1500

⏱9am-5pm Wed-Mon Nov-Feb, to 6pm Mar-May, Sep & Oct, to 6.30pm Jun-Aug

Ⓢ Line 3 to Gyeongbokgung, Exit 5

Don't Miss

Palace Layout

The palace's impressive main gate, Gwanghwa-mun, is flanked by stone carvings of *haechi*, mythical lion-like creatures. At the palace's broad front courtyard, you pass through a second gate, Heungnyemun, and over a stream to face the ornate two-storey Geunjeongjeon, an impressive throne hall where kings were crowned. West of here is Gyeonghoeru, a large pavilion resting on 48 pillars where state banquets were held.

Living Quarters & Gardens

A series of smaller meeting halls precede the king's living quarters, Gangyeongjeon, behind which are Gyotaejeon, the queen's chambers. Behind is the terraced garden, Amisan; the chimneys here released smoke from the palace's *ondol* (underfloor heating) system. On the eastern side is Donggun, the living quarters for the Crown Prince. To the rear, King Gojong built more halls for his own personal use and an ornamental pond with an attractive hexagonal pavilion (Hyangwonjeong) on an island.

Museums Within the Palace

The **National Palace Museum of Korea** (☉9am-5pm Tue-Fri, to 6pm Sat & Sun), inside Gwanghwamun, has royal artefacts that highlight the wonderful artistic skills of the Joseon era – including gold-embroidered *hanbok* (traditional clothing) worn by royalty. There's also the excellent **National Folk Museum of Korea** (www.nfm.go.kr; 37 Samcheong-ro; admission free; ☉9am-6pm Wed-Mon Mar-Oct, to 5pm Wed-Mon Nov-Feb) with three main halls covering the history of the Korean people and the life of *yangban* (aristocrats). Nearby is an open-air exhibition of early-20th-century historical buildings and structures, and the separate **National Children's Museum** (www.kidsnfm.go.kr/eng; 37 Samcheong-ro; admission free) and a play area.

☑ Top Tips

▶ Changing-of-the-guard ceremonies beside Gwanghwamun occur every hour on the hour, between 10am and 4pm.

▶ An audio commentary and a free guided tour (in English at 11am, 1.30pm and 3.30pm) are available.

▶ At the National Folk Museum of Korea the English guided tours start at 10.30am and 2.30pm, while at the National Palace Museum of Korea, the tour is at 3pm.

✗ Take a Break

Pop into the tiny but quirky Joseon Gimbap (p38) for a healthy, tasty and inexpensive lunch.

Grab a coffee and rest tired feet at **MK2** (Map p32, C2; 17 Jahamun-ro 10-gil, Jongno-gu; ☉11am-11pm; 🛜; Ⓢ Line 3 to Gyeongbokgung, Exit 5) among cool mid-century furniture.

Top Sights
Changdeokgung

The most beautiful of Seoul's four main palaces, World Heritage–listed Changdeokgung was originally built in the early 15th century as a secondary palace to Gyeongbokgung. Following the destruction of both palaces during the Japanese invasion in the 1590s, Changdeokgung was rebuilt and became the primary royal residence until 1872. It remained in use well into the 20th century.

창덕궁

◉ Map p32, G2

http://eng.cdg.go.kr/main/main.htm

99 Yulgok-ro, Jongno-gu

adult/child ₩3000/1500, plus Huwon ₩8000/4000

S Line 3 to Anguk, Exit 3

Don't Miss

Huwon (Secret Garden)

Walk through the dense woodland of the Secret Garden and suddenly you come across a serene glade. Huwon is a beautiful vista of pavilions on the edge of a square lily pond, with other halls and a two-storey library. The board out the front, written by King Jeongjo, means 'Gather the Universe'. Joseon kings relaxed, studied and wrote poems in this tranquil setting. Ongnyu-cheon is a brook at the back of the garden where there's a huge rock, Soyoam, with three Chinese characters inscribed on it by King Injo in 1636.

Injeongjeon

Enter through the imposing gate Donhwamun, dating from 1608, turn right and cross over the stone bridge (built in 1414) – note the guardian animals carved on its sides. On the left is the beautiful main palace building, Injeongjeon. It sits in harmony with the paved courtyard, the open corridors and the trees behind it. Further on are the private living quarters of the royal family. Peering inside the partially furnished rooms, you can feel what these Joseon palaces were like in their heyday – a bustling beehive buzzing round the king, full of gossip, intrigue and whispering.

Nakseonjae

Round the back of the palace is a terraced garden with decorative *ondol* chimneys. Over on the right is something completely different – Nakseonjae, built by King Heonjong (r 1834–49) in an austere Confucian style using unpainted wood. Royal descendants lived here until 1989.

☑ Top Tips

▶ You can only visit Changdeokgung on a guided tour. English tours run at 10.30am and 2.30pm; Korean tours run on the hour.

▶ Tours of Huwon are at 11.30am and 1.30pm, with an extra 3.30pm tour March to October. Book online or come early, as it's restricted to 50 people at a time.

▶ Book well ahead for monthly Moonlight Tours (₩30,000; April to June).

✗ Take a Break

Grab lunch at the elegant **Tea Museum** (Map p32, F2; ☎ 02-747 4587; www. facebook.com/TeaMuseum; 61 Changdeokgung-gil; mains ₩15,000-50,000; ⏱ 11am-8.30pm; 🛜), with meals using organic produce and views across to the palace.

Top Sights
Jogye-sa

The headquarters of the Jogye Order of Korean Buddhism has the largest hall of worship in Seoul, decorated with murals from Buddha's life and carved floral latticework doors. The temple compound, always a hive of activity, really comes alive during the city's spectacular Lotus Lantern Festival celebrating Buddha's birthday, and is a great place to learn a little about Buddhist practice.

조계사

◉ Map p32, E4

☎ 02-768 8600

www.jogyesa.kr/user/english

55-Ujeongguk-ro, Jongno-gu

⊘ 24hr

Ⓢ Line 3 to Anguk, Exit 6

Don't Miss

Daeungjeon

Inside Daeungjeon are three giant gilded Buddha statues: on the left is Amitabha, Buddha of the Western Paradise; in the centre is the historical Buddha, who lived in India and achieved enlightenment; on the right is the Bhaisaiya or Medicine Buddha, with a medicine bowl in his hand. The small 15th-century Buddha in the glass case was the main Buddha statue before he was replaced by the much larger ones in 2006.

Geuknakjeon (Paradise Hall)

Behind Daeungjeon is the modern Geuknakjeon, dedicated to Amitabha Buddha; funeral services, dharma (truth) talks and other prayer services are held here. On the left side of the compound, is the octagonal 10-storey stupa, in which is enshrined a relic of Buddha brought to Korea in 1913 by a Sri Lankan monk.

Beomjongru (Brahma Bell Pavilion)

This pavilion houses a drum to summon earth-bound animals, a wooden fish-shaped gong to summon aquatic beings, a metal cloud-shaped gong to summon birds and a large bronze bell to summon underground creatures. The bell is rung 28 times at 4am and 33 times at 6pm.

Temple Life Programs

Drop by Saturday to make a booking for the **Temple Life program** (₩30,000; ⏲1-4pm), which includes a temple tour, meditation practice, lotus-lantern and prayer-bead making, woodblock printing, painting and a tea ceremony. An overnight templestay can also be arranged here.

☑ Top Tips

▶ Believers who enter the temple bow three times, touching their forehead to the ground – once for Buddha, once for the dharma and once for the sangha (monks), 20 of whom serve in this temple.

✖ Take a Break

Treat yourself to a delicious vegetarian banquet at Balwoo Gongyang (p39).

For Korean home-cooking, **Tobang** (토방; Map p32, E3; ☎02-735 8156; 50-1 Insa-dong-gil; meals ₩6000; ⏲11.30am-9pm) has spicy stew dishes, which are eaten while sitting on cushions on the floor.

Local Life
Exploring Bukchon Hanok Village

Squished between two major palaces and rising up the foothills of Bukaksan, Bukchon is home to Seoul's largest concentration of *hanok* (traditional wooden houses). Get lost wandering its labyrinthine streets, taking in the views, and pausing at cafes, art galleries, private museums and craft shops along the way. It's best done early morning or early evening to avoid the crowds.

1 Bukchon Traditional Culture Center

To find out more about the area, head first to the **Bukchon Traditional Culture Center** (북촌문화센터; 📞02-2171 2459; http://bukchon.seoul.go.kr/eng/exp/center1_1.jsp; 37 Gyedong-gil; admission free; ⏱9am-6pm Mon-Sat; 🚇Line 3 to Anguk, Exit 3), which has a small exhibition about *hanok* and is housed, appropriately enough, in a *hanok*. Just up from here is Bukchon Tourist Information

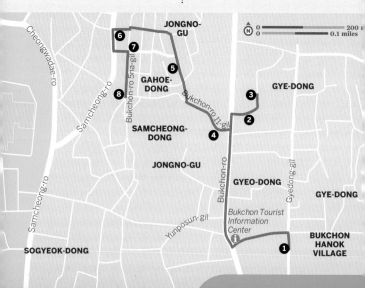

Center, with maps and leaflets about the area.

❷ Learn about Traditional Crafts

Enter **Dong-Lim Knot Workshop** (www. shimyoungmi.com; 10 Bukchon-ro 12-gil; classes from ₩1000; ☺10am-6pm Tue-Sun; Ⓢ Line 3 to Anguk, Exit 2), a lovely *hanok,* to find out about traditional knotting techniques and to attend classes on how to make tassels, jewellery and other ornaments from threads.

❸ Pop in for Folk Art

Just up from Dong-Lim Knot Workshop is **Gahoe Minhwa Workshop** (가회민화공방; ☏02-741 0466; www. gahoemuseum.org; 17 Bukchon-ro 8-gil; adult/child ₩2000/1000; ☺10.30am-6pm Tue-Sun; Ⓢ Line 3 to Anguk, Exit 2), which houses a large collection of amulets and folk paintings. This combined house-museum and cultural centre also offers classes teaching traditional painting.

❹ Pizza at Dejangjangi HwadeogPijajip

A *hanok* turned pizzeria, the friendly **Dejangjangi HwadeogPijajip** (대장 장이 화덕피자집; ☏02-765 4298; 3 Bukchon-ro 11-gil; pizza ₩14,000-20,000; ☺noon-10pm; 🛜; Ⓢ Line 3 to Anguk, Exit 2) does authentic pizzas. Dejangjangi means blacksmith and that is exactly what the owner Lee Jae-Sung is. Some of his metal creations adorn the quirky interior.

❺ Get Cultured at Simsimheon

The private body National Trust of Korea manages the residential property **Simsimheon** (심심헌; ☏02-763 3393; www.simsimheon.com; 47 Bukchon-ro 11-gil; admission ₩15,000; ☺9am-6.30pm Mon-Sat; Ⓢ Line 3 to Anguk, Exit 2), a modern *hanok* rebuilt using traditional methods. Entry includes tea, which is sipped overlooking the internal garden.

❻ Shop for Traditional Clothing

For tastefully designed, contemporary *hanbok* head to **Jilkyungyee** (질경 이; ☏02-732 5606; www.jilkyungyee.co.kr; 88 Samcheong-ro; Ⓢ Line 3 to Anguk, Exit 1), which sells everyday and special-occasion traditional Korean clothing for both sexes.

❼ Tea Time at Cha Masineun Tteul

Overlooking Samcheong-dong and Gwanghwamun is **Cha Masineun Tteul** (차마시는뜰; 26 Bukchon-ro 11na-gil; ☺10.30am-10pm; Ⓢ Line 3 to Anguk, Exit 1), a lovely *hanok* with low tables arranged around a courtyard. It serves traditional teas and a delicious bright-yellow pumpkin rice cake.

❽ Art at Another Way of Seeing

Running a program to support art education and activities for the blind, **Another Way of Seeing** (리들의 눈; ☏02-733 1996; artblind.or.kr; 19 Bukchon-ro 5na-gil; ☺10am-6pm Tue-Sun; Ⓢ Line 3 to Anguk, Exit 1) is a gallery where the thought-provoking exhibitions frequently play on senses other than sight, such as smell, touch and sound.

Cheongwadae-ro

0 — 500 m
0 — 0.25 miles

Samcheong

TONGIN-DONG
SEOCHON
10

Pirundae-ro

Jahamun-ro

TONGUI-DONG
16 21

Hyoja-ro

Gyeongbokgung

SOGYEO
DONG

MMCA
Seoul

6

12

PIRUN-
DONG
TONGUI-DONG

Sajik
Park

Sajik-ro
Gyeongbokgung

Yulgok-ro

SAJIK-
DONG

Sajik-ro 8-gil

Sejong-daero

5
National Museum of
Korean Contemporary
History

Sambong-

22

Gwanghwamun

Gwanghwamun Sq

Jong-ro

7
Gyeonghuigung
Gyeonghuigung
Park

Seoul
Museum of
History

4

Four
Seasons
Hotel

Saemunan-ro

Cheong-gye-cheon
Tourist Information
Center

2
Cheong-gye-cheon

KTO Tour
Informati
Center

13

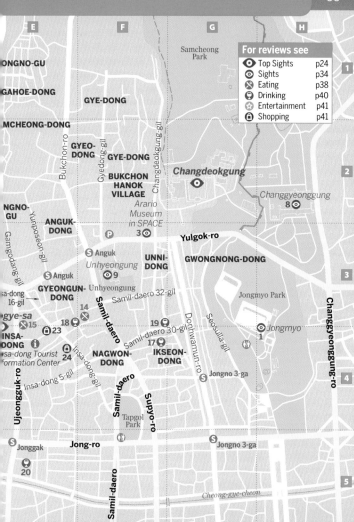

E

ONGNO-GU

GAHOE-DONG

MCHEONG-DONG

F

GYE-DONG

Bukchon-ro

GYEO-
DONG

Gyedong-gil

GYE-DONG

**BUKCHON
HANOK
VILLAGE**

*Arario
Museum
in SPACE*

Changdeokgung-gil

G

Samcheong
Park

Changdeokgung
◎

H

1

2

Changgyeonggung
8 ◎

NGNO-
GU

**ANGUK-
DONG**

Yunposeon-gil

Gamgodang-gil

sa-dong
16-gil

gye-sa

✕15

**INSA-
DONG** ℹ
sa-dong Tourist
formation Center

Ujeongguk-ro

P

3◎

🅢 Anguk
Unhyeongung
◎9

🅢 Anguk

**GYEONGUN-
DONG**

Unhyeongung

14

18 🍷

🔒23

Samil-daero

Insa-dong-gil

🔒24

Insa-dong 5-gil

**UNNI-
DONG**

Yulgok-ro

GWONGNONG-DONG

Jongmyo Park

Seosulla-gil

◎*Jongmyo*
1

3

Changgyeonggung-ro

Samil-daero 32-gil

Samil-daero 30-gil

19 🍷

17 🍷

**NAGWON-
DONG**

**IKSEON-
DONG**

Samil-daero

Supyo-ro

Donhwamun-ro

🅢

Jongno 3-ga

Jong-ro

🅢 Jonggak

🔒
20

Samil-daero

*Tapgol
Park*

🅢 Jongno 3-ga

Cheong-gye-cheon

4

5

Sights

Jongmyo
SHRINE

1  Map p32, H4

Surrounded by dense woodland, the impressive buildings of the Confucian shrine Jongmyo house the 'spirit tablets' of the Joseon kings and queens and some of their most loyal government officials. Their spirits are believed to reside in a special hole bored into the wooden tablets. For its architecture and the special ceremonies that take place here, the shrine has been awarded World Heritage status: the most famous ceremony is the **Jongmyo Daeje** in early May. (종묘; ☑ 02-765 0195; jm.cha.go.kr; 157 Jong-ro, Jongno-gu; adult/child ₩1000/500;

☺ 9am-5pm Wed-Mon Mar-Oct, to 4.30pm Wed-Mon Nov-Feb; **S** Line 1, 3 or 5 to Jongno 3-ga, Exit 11)

Cheong-gye-cheon
RIVER

2  Map p32, D5

A raised highway was torn down and cement roads removed in this US$384-million urban renewal project to 'daylight' this stream. With its landscaped walkways, footbridges, waterfalls and a variety of public artworks, such as the enormous pink-and-blue shell entitled **Spring** in **Cheong-gye Plaza**, the revitalised stream is a hit with Seoulites who come to escape the urban hubbub and, in summer, dangle their feet in the water. (청계천; www. cheonggyecheon.or.kr; 110 Sejong-daero, Jung-gu; **S** Line 5 to Gwanghwamun, Exit 5)

Arario Museum in SPACE
MUSEUM

3  Map p32, F3

Korean contemporary-art collector and business magnate Kam Chang-il has found the perfect home for jewels from his collection at this ivy-clad brick building that's considered a seminal piece of early 1970s architecture. The building's compact, low-ceilinged rooms and labyrinthine layout fit the conceptual pieces, by the likes of Nam Jun Paik, Koo Kang, Lee Ufan, Tracey Emin, Damien Hirst and Sam Taylor Johnson, like a glove – you never know what artistic wonder lies around the next corner. (☑ 02-736 5700; www.arario museum.org; 83 Yulgok-ro, Jongno-gu, 10am-7pm; adult/child/youth ₩10,000/4000/6000; **S** Line 3 to Anguk, Exit 3)

MANFRED GOTTSCHALK/GETTY IMAGES ©

Jongmyo

Cheong-gye-cheon

Seoul Museum of History

MUSEUM

4 <svg>Map p32, B5</svg>

To gain an appreciation of the total transformation of Seoul down the centuries visit this fascinating museum which charts the city's history since the dawn of the Joseon dynasty. Outside is one of the old tram cars that used to run in the city in the 1930s as well as a section of the old Gwanghwamun gate. Inside there's a massive scale model of the city you can walk around as well as donated exhibitions of crafts and photographs. (서울역사박물관; ☑02-724 0114; www.museum.seoul.kr; 55 Saemunan-ro, Jongno-gu; admission free; ☺9am-8pm Tue-Fri, to 7pm Sat & Sun; ⑤Line 5 to Gwanghwamun, Exit 7)

National Museum of Korean Contemporary History

MUSEUM

5 <svg>Map p32, D4</svg>

The last century has been a tumultuous time for Korea, the key moments of which are memorialised and celebrated in this museum charting the highs and lows of that journey. The displays are modern, multilingual and engaging, as well as proof of how far the country has come in the decades since its almost total destruction during the Korean War. (☑02-3703 9200; www.much.go.kr; 198 Sejong-daero, Jongno-gu; admission free; ☺9am-6pm Tue, Thu, Fri & Sun, to 9pm Wed & Sat; ⑤Line 5 to Gwanghwamun, Exit 2)

Top Tip

MMCA Gallery Shuttle

A free shuttle bus runs four times a day between MMCA Seoul and the other MMCA branches in Gwacheon and Deoksugung.

MMCA Seoul   MUSEUM

6 Map p32, D2

Combining architectural elements from several centuries of Seoul's history, this new branch of the city's premier contemporary-art museum is a work in progress. The melding of spacious new gallery buildings with the art deco buildings of the former Defense Security Command compound is impressive but at the time of research the facility had yet to get a director (because this is a politically sensitive appointment) and its shows have met with muted critical reaction. Nonetheless, it's well worth a visit. (02-3701 9500; www.mmca.go.kr; 30 Samcheong-ro, Jongno-gu; admission ₩4000; 10am-6pm Tue, Thu, Fri & Sun, to 9pm Wed & Sat; Line 3 to Anguk, Exit 1)

Gyeonghuigung   PALACE

7 Map p32, A4

The Palace of Shining Celebration, completed in 1623, used to consist of a warren of courtyards, buildings, walls and gates spread over a large area. But it was destroyed during the Japanese annexation and a Japanese school was established here. Only the main audience hall, **Sungjeongjeon**, and the smaller official **hall** behind it along with a few paved courtyards, walls and corridors have been restored. (경희궁; Palace of Shining Celebration; 02-724 0274; 55 Saemunan-ro; admission free; 9am-6pm Tue-Sun; Line 5 to Gwanghwamun, Exit 1)

Changgyeonggung   PALACE

8 Map p32, H2

Originally built in the early 15th century by King Sejong for his parents, the oldest surviving structure of this palace is the **Okcheongyo** stone bridge (1483) over the stream by the main gate. The main hall, **Myeongjeongjeon** (1616) has lovely latticework and an ornately carved and decorated ceiling. Look out for dates (usually in early May) when the palace is illuminated and open for night viewing, making it a romantic spot – if you can ignore the crowds. (창경궁; Palace of Flourishing Gladness; 02-762 4868; english.cha.go.kr; 185 Changgyeonggung-ro, Jongno-gu; adult/child ₩1000/500; 9am-6.30pm Tue-Sun; Line 4 to Hyehwa, Exit 4)

Unhyeongung   PALACE

9 Map p32, F3

This palace has a modest, natural-wood design reflecting the austere tastes of Heungseon Daewongun (1820–98), King Gojong's stern and conservative father. Rooms are furnished and mannequins display the dress styles of the time. It's also possible to try on *hanbok* (₩1000), and various artistic events are staged here throughout the year including traditional **music and dance concerts**, usually on Friday at noon.

Understand

Save the Hanok

- -

Endangered Species

'Thirty-five years ago there were around 800,000 *hanok* in South Korea; now there are less than 10,000', says Peter Bartholomew, an American expat in Korea. For more than 40 years Bartholomew has been battling the predominant view among Koreans that these traditional wooden houses are an anachronism in their modern country, unworthy of preserving.

Bartholomew has lived in *hanok* since he first came to Korea in 1968 as a Peace Corps volunteer and has owned one in the Dongsomun-dong area of northern Seoul since 1974. In 2009 Bartholomew and his neighbours won a two-year legal battle against the city over plans to redevelop the area. 'I deplore the assumption that these old houses are irreparable, dirty and unsanitary', he says, pointing out that traditional *hanok* are very easy to modernise in just the same way that centuries-old homes across the West have been adapted to contemporary life.

The proof of this lies in the Bukchon area, where some 900 *hanok* remain, the bulk concentrated in a few streets in Gahoe-dong. 'The preservation program has only been achieved by the government providing financial incentives to owners for repairs and maintenance', says Bartholomew. However, according to some local residents, even in Bukchon the *hanok* as a private home is under threat. Kahoi-dong 'is being relentlessly destroyed', says David Kilburn, author of Preservation of Kahoi-dong (www.kahoidong.com), a website that documents the abuses of the preservation system over the past decade.

Tourist Attraction

Contemporary Seoulites may shun *hanok* as places to live, but tourists clearly love them if the increasing number of *hanok* guesthouses is anything to go by. Ahn Young-hwan, owner of Rak-Ko-Jae, a *hanok* guesthouse in Bukchon, was one of the first people to suggest that *hanok* be used in this way. 'People thought I was crazy', he says, 'but now many more people are doing it'.

For Ahn, *hanok* are the 'vessels that contain Korean culture' and a way of experiencing the joys of an analogue life in an increasingly digital society. It's a view that Bartholomew underlines when he says that living in his *hanok* has 'filled my life with peace and beauty'.

(운현궁; ☎02-766 9090; www.unhyeongung.
or.kr; 464 Samil-daero; adult/child ₩700/300;
⊙9am-7pm Tue-Sun Apr-Oct, to 6pm Tue-Sun
Nov-Mar; **S**Line 3 to Anguk, Exit 4)

Eating

Tongin Market
Box Lunch Cafe   KOREAN $

10 Map p32, B2

For a fun lunch, buy 10 brass coins
(₩5000) at the cafe about halfway
along this old-school covered market.
You'll be given a plastic tray with
which you can then go shopping in
the market. Exchange your coins for
dishes such as savoury pancakes, *gimbap* (seaweed-covered rice rolls) and
tteokbokki (spicy rice-cake stew). (통
인시장; tonginmarket.co.kr; 18 Jahamun-ro
15-gil, Jongno-gu; meals ₩5000; ⊙11am-4pm
Tue-Sun; **S**Line 3 to Gyeongbokgung, Exit 2)

Joseon Gimbap   KOREAN $

11 Map p32, D2

Behind the new contemporary-art museum, this quirky, tiny place has astro

Local Life
Koong
The traditional Kaeseong-style
dumplings at **Koong** (Map p32, E3; 궁;
www.koong.co.kr; 11-3 Insa-dong 10-gil;
dumplings ₩10,000; ⊙11.30am-9.30pm;
SLine 3 to Anguk, Exit 6) are legendary. They're big, so only order one
portion, unless you're superhungry.

turf in the front seating area where
you get a ring-side seat on the jumbo
gimbap being made. These whop-
pers come with a range of side dishes
making it one of the best-value feeds
in the city. (조선김밥; 78 Yulgok-ro 1-gil,
Jongno-gu; gimbap ₩3500; ⊙11am-2.30pm
& 4.30-7.30pm Mon-Sat; **S**Line 3 to Anguk,
Exit 1)

Tosokchon   KOREAN $$

12 Map p32, B3

Spread over a series of *hanok*, Tosokchon is so famous for its *samgyetang*
(ginseng chicken soup) that there is
always a long queue waiting to get
in, particularly at weekends. Try the
black chicken version which uses the
silkie breed with naturally black flesh
and bones. (토속촌; ☎02-737 7444; 5
Jahamun-ro 5-gil; mains ₩15,000-22,000;
⊙10am-10pm; **S**Line 3 to Gyeongbokgung,
Exit 2)

Congdu   KOREAN $$$

13 Map p32, C5

Feast on elegantly presented, contemporary twists on Korean classics, such
as pinenut soup with soy milk espuma
(foam) or raw blue crab, at this serene
restaurant tucked away behind the
British embassy. The main dining
room becomes an open roof terrace
in good weather. (www.congdu.com; 116-1
Deoksugung-gil, Jung-gu; set course lunch/
dinner from ₩36,800/58,800; mains from
₩29,800; ⊙11.30am-1.50pm & 5.30-8.30pm;
SLine 5 to Gwanghwamun, Exit 6)

Gyeonghuigung (p36)

Min's Club
FUSION $$$

14  Map p32, F3

Old-world architecture meets new-world cuisine in this classy restaurant housed in a beautifully restored turn-of-the-20th-century *hanok*, said to be the first in Seoul to incorporate Western features such as private bathrooms. The European-Korean meals (more European than Korean) are beautifully presented and there's an extensive wine selection. (민가 다헌; ☑02-733 2966; www.minsclub. co.kr; 23-9 Insa-dong 10-gil, Jongno-gu; set course lunch/dinner from ₩32,000/70,000; ⊗noon-2.30pm & 6-9.30pm; Ⓢ Line 3 to Anguk, Exit 6)

Balwoo Gongyang
VEGETARIAN $$$

15 Map p32, E3

Reserve three days in advance for the delicate temple-style cuisine served here. Take your time to fully savour the subtle flavours and different textures of the vegetarian dishes, which range from rice porridge and delicate salads to dumplings and fried shitake mushrooms and mugwort in a sweet and sour sauce. (발우공 양; ☑02-2031 2081; www.balwoogongyang. or.kr; 5th fl, Templestay Information Center, 56 Ujeongguk-ro, Jongno-gu; lunch/dinner from ₩27,500/39,600; ⊗11.40am-3pm & 6-8.50pm; ☑; Ⓢ Line 3 to Anguk, Exit 6)

GastroTong
SWISS, EUROPEAN $$$

16 Map p32, B2

Swiss-German chef Roland Hinni and his wife Yong-Shin run this charming gourmet restaurant that blends sophistication with traditional European cooking. The set lunches are splendid deals, including appetiser, soup or salad, dessert and drinks as well as a wide choice of main courses. It's small so booking is essential. (☑02-730 4162; www.gastrotong.co.kr; 1-36 Jahamun-ro 6-gil; set course lunch/dinner from ₩30,000/50,000; ⏲noon-3pm & 6-8.30pm; 🛜; S Line 3 to Gyeongbokgung, Exit 3)

Drinking

Sik Mool
BAR

17 Map p32, F4

Four *hanok* were creatively combined to create this chic designer cafe-bar that blends old and new Seoul. Clay tile walls, Soviet-era propaganda posters, mismatched modern furniture and contemporary art surround a young crowd

Local Life
Story of the Blue Star

A much-loved Insa-dong hang-out, the divey **Story of the Blue Star** (Map p32, E3; 푸른별 주막; ☑02-734 3095; 17-1 Insa-dong 16-gil, Jongno-gu; ⏲3pm-midnight; S Line 3 to Anguk, Exit 6) is an atmospheric place to sample *makgeolli* (milky rice wine) served out of brass kettles.

sipping cocktails, coffee and wine and nibbling on house-made pizza. (식물; ☑02-747 4858; 46-1 Donhwamun-ro 11da-gil, Jongno-gu; ⏲11am-midnight; S Line 1, 3 or 5 to Jongno 3-ga, Exit 6)

Dawon
TEAHOUSE

18 Map p32, E3

The perfect place to unwind under the shady fruit trees in a courtyard with flickering candles. In colder weather sit indoors in *hanok* rooms decorated with scribbles or in the garden pavilion. The teas are superb, especially *omijacha hwachae* (fruit and five-flavour berry punch), a summer drink. (다원; ☑02-730 6305; 11-4 Insa-dong 10-gil, Jongno-gu; teas ₩7000; ⏲10.30am-10.30pm; S Line 3 to Anguk, Exit 6)

Brew 3.14
BAR

19 Map p32, F3

Along with sibling operation Brew 3.15 across the road, Brew 3.14 has carved a name for itself with its great selection of local craft beers, delicious pizza (which they call by the American name 'pie') and moreish fried chicken. Both bars are quiet, convivial places to hang out over pints and eats. (☑070-4178 3014; www.facebook.com/brew314; 39 Donhwamun-ro 11-gil, Jongno-gu; ⏲4pm-midnight; S Line 1, 3 or 5 to Jongno 3-ga, Exit 6)

Baekseju-maeul
BAR

20 Map p32, E5

From the floor seating area there's a dress circle view of the Bosingak pavilion. See the website's English pages to learn more about the excellent range of traditional rice wines available at this drinking and dining outlet for brewer Kooksoondang. (백세주마을; ☎02-720 0055; www.ksdb.co.kr; 10 Ujeongguk-ro 2-gil; ⏱5pm-1am; ⑤Line 2 to Jonggak, Exit 4)

Hopscotch BAR

 21 Map p32, B2

The prime appeal of this gastropub is its location in a converted *hanok,* which makes for a cosy spot to sample its range of local and international microbrews. The US comfort food is very tasty but served in small portions and on the pricey side. (☎02-722 0145; www.hopscotch.co.kr; 14-1 Hyoja-ro 7-gil, Jongno-gu; ⏱5pm-1am Mon-Fri, 11.30am-9pm Sat & Sun; ⑤Line 3 to Gyeongbokgung, Exit 4)

Entertainment

Sejong Center for the Performing Arts THEATRE

 22 Map p32, C4

One of Seoul's leading arts complexes with several performance and exhibition spaces puts on major drama, music and art shows – everything from large-scale musicals to fusion *gugak* (traditional Korean music) and chamber orchestras. (세종문화회관; ☎02-399 1114; www.sejongpac.or.kr; 175 Sejong-daero; ⑤Line 5 to Gwanghwamun, Exit 1 or 8)

Shopping

KCDF Gallery CRAFTS

 23 Map p32, E4

The Korean Craft and Design Foundation's gallery has a shop on the ground floor showcasing some of the finest locally made products including woodwork, pottery and jewellery. It's the ideal place to find a unique, sophisticated gift or souvenir. (☎02-793 9041; www.kcdf.kr; 8 Insa-dong 11-gil, Jongno-gu; ⏱10am-7pm; ⑤Line 3 to Anguk, Exit 6)

Insa-dong Maru CRAFTS

 24 Map p32, E4

Around 60 different Korean designer shops selling crafts, fashion and homewares are gathered at this slick, new complex spread over several levels around a central rest area where there's a piano available for impromptu concerts by passers-by. (☎02-2223 2500; www.insadongmaru. co.kr; 35-4 6 Insa-dong-gil, Jongno-gu; ⏱10.30am-8.30pm Sun-Fri, to 9pm Sat; ⑤Line 3 to Anguk, Exit 6)

Local Life
Northern Seoul

Getting There

S Line 4 to Hyehwa, Exit 2

The city's northern districts are home to some of Seoul's most charming neighbourhoods, and includes some of the best sections of the city walls. Wander the vibrant alleyways of the mural village at Ihwa before hitting parklands and the university district of Daehangno, a performing-arts hub with some 150 theatres.

❶ Street Art at Ihwa Maeul

High on the slopes of Naksan, **Ihwa Maeul** (이화 벽화 마을; Ihwa-dong) is one of the city's old *daldongnae* (literally 'moon villages'), where refugees lived in shacks after the Korean War. Sixty years later it has morphed into a tourism hotspot thanks to a growing collection of quirky sculptures and imaginative murals on walls along the village's steep stairways and alleys. Come early in the day – unless you like being surrounded by mobs carrying selfie sticks.

❷ Views from On the Hill Cafe

Beside the flowers-on-the-steps mural in Ihwa Maeul, **On the Hill Cafe** (☑02-743 7044; 68-7 Yulgok-ro 19-gil; ⏰10.30am-10.30pm; 🛜) is a good spot for a breather and has a broad outdoor terrace providing fine over-the-rooftops vistas, which are particularly pleasant around sunset.

❸ Take a Stroll in Naksan Park

On the slopes above Daehangno, **Naksan Park** (낙산공원; parks.seoul.go.kr; 54 Naksan-gil) provides fantastic views of the city and contains an impressive section of the Seoul City Wall that you can follow in either direction (and often on both sides) between Dongdaemun and Seongbuk-dong.

❹ Lock Museum

One of Seoul's quirkier private collections, the **Lock Museum** (쇳대박물관; ☑02-766 6494; 100 Ihwajang-gil; adult/child ₩4000/3000; ⏰10am-6pm Tue-Sun) makes for a surprisingly absorbing exhibition. It focuses on the artistry of locks, latches and keys of all kinds, mainly from Korea but also with international examples, including a gruesome-looking chastity belt.

❺ Galleries at Arko Art Centre

Interesting, often avant-garde art is assembled in three large galleries at **Arko Art Centre** (아르코미술관; ☑02-760 4850; www.arkoartcenter.or.kr/nr3; 3 Dongsung-gil; ⏰11am-7pm; FREE), run by the Arts Council Korea. The big red-brick complex (designed by Kim Swoo-geun, one of Korea's most famous postwar architects) overlooks Marronnier Park.

❻ Performances at Marronnier

The free performance area and sculptures at **Marronnier Park** (마로니에공원; 104 Daehak-ro) usually have something happening on afternoons and evenings on the outdoor stage.

❼ Culture Events ArkoPAC

In the large industrial **ArkoPAC** (☑02-3668 0007; www.koreapac.kr; 17 Daehak-ro 10-gil) complex, designed by Kim Swoo-geun, are the main and small halls of both the Arko Art Theatre and Daehangno Arts Theatre. Come here for a varied dance-oriented program of events and shows.

❽ Refreshments at Hakrim

Little has changed in this retro Seoul classic since **Hakrim** (www.hakrim.pe.kr; 119 Daehak-ro, Jongno-gu; ⏰10am-midnight; 🛜; ⓈLine 4 to Hyehwa, Exit 3) opened in 1956, save for the price of drinks. Apart from coffee, it also serves tea and alcohol.

Explore

Myeong-dong & Jung-gu

Seoul's retail world bursts forth in the bright neon-lit, packed-to-the-gills and noisy streets of Myeong-dong. It's home to the massive 24-hour Namdaemun Market, Korea's largest. Looming over the commercial frenzy are the peaceful and tree-clad slopes of Namsan, a great place for exercise and city views. Its downtown area offers outstanding sightseeing, with colonial architecture and Deoksugung palace.

The Sights in a Day

☀ Get your morning exercise by walking up the scenic slopes of **Namsan** (p46); or alternatively journey up via cable car. Head up **N Seoul Tower** (p46) for wonderful city views, before taking the walking path back to town, ending up at **Namdaemun Market** (p48) for tasty Korean food.

☀ Shop for handicrafts at the sprawling market, and cross the road to admire the Joseon-era **Sungnyemun** (p49; pictured left). Take a walk to downtown Seoul and drop by the **Seoul Museum of Art** (p55). Then meander off to **Deoksugung** (p50), timing your visit for the changing-of-the-guard ceremony. Afterwards head across to check out **Seoul City Hall's** (p54) striking facade and exhibitions.

☾ Take a break and grab a bite (and beer) at **A Person** (p58) before venturing back to Deoksugung to see its buildings eerily illuminated at night. Jump on the subway to Myeong-dong's **shopping district** (p62) to soak up the atmosphere of its buzzing streets ablaze with neon.

 Top Sights

Namsan & N Seoul Tower (p46)

Namdaemun Market (p48)

Deoksugung (p50)

💜 **Best of Seoul**

Eating

Gosang (p60)

Korea House (p62)

Gogung (p59)

Drinking

Craftworks (p60)

Entertainment

Nanta Theatre (p61)

National Theatre of Korea (p62)

Shopping

Shinsegae (p62)

Lotte Department Store (p63)

Lab 5 (p63)

Åland (p63)

Getting There

S **Subway** Line 4 to Myeong-dong, or Line 1 or 2 to City Hall.

Top Sights
Namsan & N Seoul Tower

Beloved by locals as a place for exercise, peaceful contemplation and hanging out with loved ones, Namsan was a sacred shamanistic spot when the Joseon ruler Taejo ordered the construction of a city wall across this and Seoul's three other guardian mountains. The mountain is protected within a 109-hectare park and crowned by one of the city's most iconic features: N Seoul Tower.

👁 Map p52, E5

www.nseoultower.com

adult/child ₩9000/7000

🕙10am-11pm

🚌shuttle buses 2, 3, 5

Namsan cable car

Don't Miss

N Seoul Tower

The iconic N Seoul tower (236m), the geographic centre of Seoul, sits atop the city's guardian mountain, Namsan. The panoramic views of Seoul from its observation deck are immense. The tower has become a hot date spot with the railings around it festooned with locks inscribed with lovers' names. Walking up Namsan isn't hard, but riding the **cable car** (one-way adult/child ₩6000/3000, return adult/child ₩8500/5500) is popular for the views.

City Wall & Bongsudae

Sections of the original Seoul City Wall still snake across Namsan; near the summit you can also see the **Bongsudae** (signal beacons), which were used for 500 years to notify the central government of urgent political and military information. A traditional lighting ceremony is held here between 3pm and 4pm Tuesday to Sunday.

Northern Namsan Circuit

Along the Northern Namsan Circuit, a pedestrian path snakes for 3km from the lower cable-car station to the National Theatre. Walking alongside the restored city wall, you'll find the ornate and peaceful **Waryongmyo** (⏱8am-4pm). Built in 1862, this Buddhist/Taoist/shamanist shrine is dedicated to Zhuge Liang (AD 181–234), a Chinese statesman and general.

Southern Namsan Circuit

The Southern Namsan Circuit has a pedestrian path and a road used by buses. It cuts through the old Seoul City Wall. Accessed from the Southern Namsan Circuit or via a footbridge over the road from near the Grand Hyatt is the Namsan Outdoor Botanical Garden. From here paths lead through more wooded sections of Namsan Park.

☑ Top Tips

▶ Come at sunset and you can watch the city morph into a galaxy of twinkling stars. Book ahead if you want to eat at N Seoul Tower's revolving restaurant.

▶ If you're here for exercise, tack on a session of free weights at the open-air gym on the northern section. Further along is an archery practice ground where you can practise firing arrows.

✗ Take a Break

A wonderful spot for a traditional Korean lunch is Mokmyeoksanbang (p58), an attractive leafy restaurant on on Namsan's slopes.

If you want to treat yourself, book ahead to dine at N.Grill (p60), a revolving French restaurant atop N Seoul Tower.

Top Sights
Namdaemun Market & Around

You could spend all day in this swarming night-and-day market and not see it at all. The largest market in South Korea, each section has hundreds of stalls, from clothing and handicrafts to accessories. It can be a confusing place; get your bearings from the numbered gates on the periphery. Its helpful **tourist information centre** (📞02-752 1913; Gate 5 or 7; 🕙10am-7pm) has a good map.

👁 Map p52, C3

www.namdaemunmarket.co.kr

21 Namdaemunsijang 4-gil, Jung-gu

🕙24hr

Ⓢ Line 4 to Hoehyeon, Exit 5

Don't Miss

Shopping

Haggling is the mode of business at this large overwhelming market. For Korean souvenirs head to the wholesale handicrafts section of Joongang Building C and D (Gate 2; ◷7am-6pm Mon-Fri, to 2pm Sat), where there's also traditional Korean cookware, such as bowls, plates and eating utensils – perfect for those dinner parties back home. **Samho Woojoo** (Gate 3; ◷7am-5pm Mon-Sat) has a jaw-dropping amount of fashion jewellery, while camera shops are clustered near Gate 1.

Food Alleys

Eating is one of the highlights of visiting Namdaemun. From lively hole-in-the-wall eateries to outdoor stalls, the cooking is all fresh and tasty. Specialities include *sujebi* (dough and shellfish soup), homemade *kalguksu* (noodles in a meat, dumpling and vegetable broth) or bibimbap. A bottle of *makgeolli* (milky rice wine) rounds out the experience. Also look out for street vendors famous for vegie *hotteok* (deep-fried pancakes) and other tasty snacks to go.

Sungnyemun

Standing alone on an island – in direct contrast to the mayhem around it – is Seoul's picturesque Great South Gate, **Sungnyemun** (남대문, Namdaemun; www.sungnyemun.or.kr; admission free; ◷9am-6pm Tue-Sun). One of the capital's original four main gates, it was built in the 14th century. Its arched brick entrance, topped by a double-storey pavilion, is accessed by a pedestrian crossing from Gate 1 of Namdaemun Market. It's been reconstructed a number of times over the years following damage from Japanese occupation and the Korean War, plus it underwent a painstaking four-year reconstruction recently after an arson attack in 2008.

☑ Top Tips

▶ Consider doing your souvenir shopping here, with good discounts on the same items you'll find in Insa-dong.

▶ Different sections have different opening hours and some shops open on Sunday, although that's not the best time to visit.

✗ Take a Break

There are plenty of places to take a breather at this expansive market. For bibimbab (₩5000) head to the stalls clustered near Gate 5 on **Kalguksu Alley**. For proper sit-down restaurants head to **Haejangguk Alley**, between Gates 2 and 3. Next to Gate 2 is a great stall selling vegie *hotteok* (₩1000) and toasted sandwiches filled with egg, ham and cheese (₩1700).

Top Sights
Deoksugung

One of Seoul's five grand palaces built during the Joseon dynasty, Deoksugung (meaning Palace of Virtuous Longevity) is the only one you can visit in the evening and see the buildings illuminated. It served as a palace from 1593, yet became a secondary residence. It became a primary residence again in 1897 when King Gojong moved in and remained so until the early-20th-century Japanese occupation. It's a fascinating mix of traditional Korean and Western-style neoclassical structures.

덕수궁

⊙ Map p52, B2

www.deoksugung.go.kr

99 Sejong-daero, Jung-gu

adult/under 7yr/child ₩1000/free/500

⊙ 9am-9pm Tue-Sun

Ⓢ Line 1 or 2 to City Hall, Exit 2

Changing of the Guard ceremony

Don't Miss

Architecture

Deoksugung is a potpourri of contrasting architectural styles. Junghwajeon, the palace's main throne hall, was used for ceremonial occasions such as coronations, and is adorned with dragons and golden window frames. Behind it is the monumental neoclassical-style Seokjojeon, designed by British architect GR Harding and completed in 1910. Its equally grand western wing was designed by a Japanese architect in 1938. Jeonggwanheon is the interesting fusion-style pavilion designed by Russian architect Aleksey Seredin-Sabatin as a place for the emperor to savour coffee and entertain guests.

Changing of the Guard

The changing of the guard is an impressive ceremony involving 50 participants, who dress up as Joseon-era soldiers and bandsmen. It happens at the Daehanmun main gate three times a day at 11am, 2pm and 3.30pm Tuesday to Sunday.

Museums

Within Seokjojeon is the **Daehan Empire History Museum** (✆02-751 0753; www.deoksugung.go.kr; Deoksugung; admission free; ◷9.30am-5pm Tue-Sun), which displays the mansion's opulent interior. You can only visit as part of a 45-minute tour, best booked online (though it's not in English), or otherwise chance your luck upon arrival; tours depart approximately every half-hour until 5pm. The western wing is now the MMCA Deoksugun**g**, featuring a collection of permanent and temporary contemporary art.

☑ Top Tips

▸ For a more unique and peaceful atmosphere visit in the evening when the buildings are illuminated and crowds thin out.

▸ Free guided tours of the palace (in English) take place at 10.30am and 1.30pm Tuesday to Friday, and at 1.30pm on weekends. Otherwise, you can pick up a detailed guide for ₩500.

✖ Take a Break

For those visiting in the evening or late afternoon, A Person (p58) is good spot for a break with burritos and craft beer.

A 10-minute walk from the palace, Soo:P Coffee Flower (p59) does gourmet sandwiches, light Korean mains and excellent coffee.

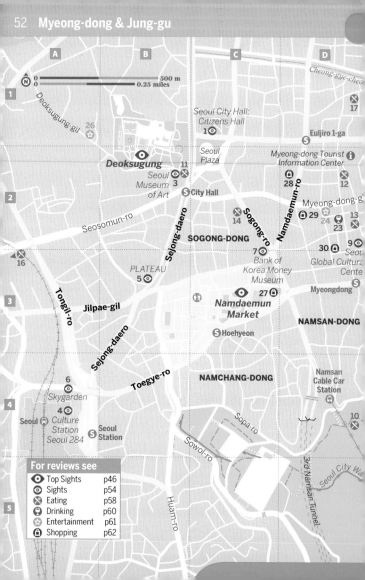

A B C D

N 0   500 m
  0   0.25 miles

1

Deoksugung-gil

26

2

Seoul City Hall;
Citizens Hall
1

Cheong-gye-cheo

17

Euljiro 1-ga

Seoul
Plaza

Myeong-dong Tourist
Information Center

28

Myeong-dong-g

Deoksugung
Seoul
Museum
of Art

11
3

City Hall

12

29

24 13
23

Seosomun-ro

14

SOGONG-DONG

Sogong-ro

Namdaemun-ro

30

9
Seou
Global Cultura
Cente

3

PLATEAU
5

Bank of
Korea Money
Museum

7

27

Myeongdong

Jilpae-gil

Namdaemun
Market

NAMSAN-DONG

Tongil-ro

16

Hoehyeon

Sejong-daero

Sejong-daero

Toegye-ro

6
Skygarden

NAMCHANG-DONG

Namsan
Cable Car
Station

4

Seoul
Culture
Station
Seoul 284

4
Seoul
Station

Sopa-ro

Sowol-ro

10

3rd Namsan Tunnel

Seoul City Wa

Huam-ro

For reviews see

⊙	Top Sights	p46
⊙	Sights	p54
✕	Eating	p58
🍴	Drinking	p60
★	Entertainment	p61
🔒	Shopping	p62

5

E
F
G
H

Samil-daero
🚇 20

1

Euljiro 3-ga
Ⓢ

JUNG-GU
Euljiro 4-ga
Ⓢ

Eulji-ro
🚇 19

Supyo-ro

Chungmu-ro

Mareunnae-ro

INHYUNG-DONG

Changgyeonggung-ro

Dongho-ro

2

22
🚇
Myeong-dong
Catholic Cathedral

15
❌

Samil-daero

ungmuro

Toegye-ro

Ⓢ Chungmuro

3

Seoul
nimation
Center ⊙ 8

YEJANG-DONG

Dongguk
University Ⓢ

21
🚇

Sopa-ro

2 ⊙
Namsangol
Hanok Village

Dongguk
University

Northern Namsan Circuit

Time
Capsule
Sq

4

Namsan
Park

JUNG-GU

1st Namsan Tunnel

2nd Namsan Tunnel

Jangchungdan-ro

25
☆

5

Upper Cable
Car Station
🚇
Namsan &
◉ N Seoul Tower
❌18

Sights

Seoul City Hall
ARCHITECTURE

1 ◎ Map p52, C1

Looking like a tsunami made of glass and steel, the Seoul City Hall was completely redeveloped in 2013. It is a modern reinterpretation of traditional Korean design; the cresting wave providing shade (like eaves found on palaces and temple roofs) over the handsome old City Hall which was built from stone in 1926. (서울시청사; http://english.seoul.go.kr; 110 Sejong-daero, Jung-gu; admission free; ⏰7.30am-6pm Mon-Fri, from 9am Sat & Sun; ⑤Line 1 or 2 to City Hall, Exit 5)

Local Life

Seoul Plaza & Library

The grassy **Seoul Plaza** (Map p52, C2; ⑤Line 1 or 2 to City Hall, Exit 5) has been a gathering spot for everything from democracy protests to major events such as the 2002 World Cup. It's also the scene for events and free performances during the summer, as well as an outdoor ice-skating rink for a couple of months each winter. Looming over it is **Seoul Metropolitan Library** (Map p52, C1; http://lib.seoul.go.kr; 110 Sejong-daero, Jung-gu; ⏰9am-9pm; ⑤Lines 1 or 2 to City Hall, Exit 5), which is within the original City Hall reniassance-style building constructed in 1926 and fronted by its iconic clock. As well as a public library, there are photography exhibitions relating to Seoul's history.

Namsangol Hanok Village
CULTURAL CENTRE

2 ◎ Map p52, F3

Located in a park at the foot of Namsan, this peaceful village is a wonderful spot to encounter traditional Korean culture. It features five differing *yangban* (upper-class) houses from the Joseon era, all relocated here from different parts of Seoul. Also here is **Seoul Namsan Gugakdang** (☎02-2261 0512; tickets from ₩20,000; ⏰closed Tue; ⑤Line 3 or 4 to Chungmuro, Exit 4), where traditional music and concerts are staged most evenings. On the right of the entrance gate is an office that provides free hour-long tour guides around the village at 10.30am, noon, 2pm and 3.30pm. (남산골한옥마을; ☎02-2264 4412; http://hanokmaeul.or.kr; 28 Toegye-ro 34-gil; admission free; ⏰9am-9pm Wed-Mon Apr-Oct, to 8pm Wed-Mon Nov-Mar, office 10am-5pm; ⑤Line 3 or 4 to Chungmuro, Exit 4)

Citizens Hall
CULTURAL CENTRE

Head down City Hall's basement to reach Citizens Hall (see 1 ◎ Map p52, C1) , a mulitpurpose space with an interesting mix of multimedia art exhibitions, design shops and a fair-trade cafe. There's also a 21st-century version of Speakers Corner and Media Wall where locals can express their views. Pick up a map and guide from its information desk. (☎02-739 7733; www.seoulcitizenshall.kr; basement, City Hall, 110 Sejong-daero, Jung-gu; admission free; ⏰9am-9pm Tue-Sun; ⑤Line 1 or 2 to City Hall, Exit 5)

45

Seoul City Hall

Seoul Museum of Art   GALLERY

3 ◉ Map p52, B2

Hosting world-class exhibitions that
are always worth a visit, this museum
has ultramodern, bright galleries
inside the handsome brick-and-stone
facade of the 1928 Supreme Court
building. For some special exhibitions

Top Tip

Seoul City Walking Tours

With three days advance notice, you
can arrange a free guided tour of the
area (and other neighbourhoods of
Seoul) with a volunteer from **Seoul
City Walking Tours** (☎02-6925 0777;
http://dobo.visitseoul.net).

an entrance fee is charged. (서울시
립미술관; SEMA; ☎02-2124 8800; www.
sema.seoul.go.kr/; 61 Deoksugung-gil, Jung-
gu; admission free; ⊙10am-8pm Tue-Fri,
to 7pm Sat & Sun; Ⓢ Line 1 or 2 to City Hall,
Exit 2)

Culture Station
Seoul 284   ARCHITECTURE, GALLERY

4 ◉ Map p52, A4

This grand 1925 building with a
domed roof has been beautifully restored inside and out and made into a
cultural-arts space staging a variety of
events. The number 284 refers to the
station's historic site number. (www.
seoul284.org; 426 Cheongpa-ro, Jung-gu;
admission free; ⊙10am-7pm Tue-Sun; Ⓢ Line
1 or 4 to Seoul Station, Exit 2)

Local Life

Myeong-dong Catholic Cathedral

Go inside the elegant, red- and grey-brick Gothic-style **Myeong-dong Catholic Cathedral** (명동 성당; Map p52, E2; ☎02-774 1784; www.mdsd.or.kr; 74 Myeong-dong-gil, Jung-gu; admission free; ⑤Line 4 to Myeongdong, Exit 6), consecrated in 1898, to admire the vaulted ceiling and stained-glass windows. The cathedral provided a sanctuary for student and trade-union protestors during military rule, becoming a national symbol of democracy and human rights. Its sleek modern plaza entrance adds an intriguing 21st-century touch.

PLATEAU
GALLERY

5 ◎ Map p52, B3

Sponsored by Samsung, and formerly known as the Rodin Gallery, this unusual glass pavilion was built to house castings of two monumental sculptures by Auguste Rodin: *The Gates of Hell* and *The Burgers of Calais*. Changing contemporary art exhibitions are staged in two additional gallery spaces. (www.plateau.or.kr; 150 Taepyeong-no 2-ga, Jung-gu; adult/child ₩3000/2000; ⏰10am-6pm Tue-Sun; ⑤Line 1 or 2 to City Hall, Exit 8)

Skygarden
PARK

6 ◎ Map p52, A4

Earmarked for completion by the end of 2017, Seoul's Skygarden is proposed to be what the High Line is to New York, an elevated urban tree-filled park in the heart of the city. It will run along an abandoned stretch of highway overpass near Seoul Station. (Seoul Station; ⑤Line 1 or 4 to Seoul Station, Exit 2)

Bank of Korea Money Museum
MUSEUM

7 ◎ Map p52, C3

Built in 1912, and an outstanding example of Japanese colonial architecture, the old Bank of Korea now houses a reasonably interesting exhibition on the history of local and foreign currency. There's plenty of interactive displays for kids, such as being able to press your own coin or test for counterfeit notes. (☎02-759 4881; www.museum.bok.or.kr; 39 Namdaemun-ro, Jung-gu; admission free; ⏰10am-5pm Tue-Sun; ♿; ⑤Line 4 to Hoehyeon, Exit 7)

Seoul Animation Center
MUSEUM

8 ◎ Map p52, E3

Up the hill on the way to the cable car you'll find this museum and cinema devoted to cartoons and animation from Korea and beyond. (서울애니메 이션센터; www.ani.seoul.kr; 126 Sopa-ro, Jung-gu; admission free; ⏰9am-5.50pm Tue-Sun; ⑤Line 4 to Myeongdong, Exit 1 or 3)

Seoul Global Cultural Center
CULTURAL TOUR

9 ◎ Map p52, D2

Set up to promote Korean culture to foreigners, this centre offers classes in anything from *hanji* (handmade

Understand

Seoul During the Korean War

Through the ages there has been no shortage of internal conflict on the Korean Peninsula. The Korean War (1950–53) represents another such conflict along internally riven lines. On 25 June 1950, under the cover of night, the North Korean army marched over the mountains that rim Seoul, marking the start of the brutal civil war.

Seoul's sudden fall to the North caught the populace by surprise; the government of President Syngman Rhee fled southward, destroying the only Han River highway bridge and leaving the remaining population to face the communists. During its 90-day occupation of the city, North Korea's army arrested and shot many who had supported the Rhee government.

In September 1950, UN forces led by US and South Korean troops mounted a counterattack. After an amphibious landing at Incheon, they fought their way back into Seoul. During a series of bloody battles, whole districts of the capital were bombed and burned in the effort to dislodge Kim II Sung's Korean People's Army. When at last UN forces succeeded in reclaiming the city, much of it lay in smouldering ruins.

Later that year, as UN forces pushed northward, the Chinese Army entered the war on the North Korean side and pushed back down into Seoul. This time the invaders found a nearly empty city. Even after the UN regained control in March 1951, only a fraction of Seoul's population returned during the two years of war that raged along the battle-front until the armistice in July 1953. Instead, they holed up in rural villages and miserable camps, slowly trickling back into the shattered capital that was once their home.

Widespread hunger, disease, crime and misery comprised daily life for hundreds of thousands of people. On the slopes of Namsan a wretched village called Haebang-chon (Liberation Town) housed tens of thousands of war refugees, widows and beggars. Prostitutes lined up at the gates of the US military bases in Yongsan in a desperate effort to earn a few dollars. Even a decade after the war, average male life expectancy hovered barely above 50.

paper) craft, painting and calligraphy, to Korean film screenings, photo ops wearing traditional clothing or K-Pop dance lessons (₩5000, 1½ hours). Most activities are free; visit the website for schedules and events. (☏02-3789 7961; www.seoulculturalcenter. com; 5th fl, M-Plaza Bldg, 27 Myeongdong 8-gil, Jung-gu; ☺10.30am-7.30pm; §Line 4 to Myeongdong, Exit 6)

Eating

Mokmyeoksanbang   KOREAN $

10 Map p52, D4

Order and pay at the till, then pick up delicious and beautifully presented bibimbap from the kitchen when your electronic buzzer rings. The traditional wooden house in which the restaurant is based is named after the ancient name for Namsan (Mokmyeok); it also serves Korean teas and *makgeolli* (rice wine) in brass kettles. (목멱산방;

 Local Life
Myeong-dong Gyoja
The special *kalguksu* (noodles in a meat, dumpling and vegetable broth) at **Myeong-dong Gyoja** (명동교자; Map p52, E2; www.mdkj.co.kr; 29 Myeongdong 10-gil, Jung-gu; noodles ₩8000; ☺10.30am-9.30pm; §Line 4 to Myeongdong, Exit 8) are an institution, so it's busy, busy, busy. Fortunately it has multiple levels and a nearby branch to meet the demand.

Northern Namsan Circuit, Jung-gu; mains ₩8000-10,000; ☺11.30am-8pm; §Line 4 to Myeongdong, Exit 3)

A Person   MEXICAN $

11 Map p52, B2

A cool little spot with stencil art and comic-book-themed murals on its walls, this basement den does tasty pork-belly and shrimp burritos, matched perfectly with Korean craft beers. (Taepyeong-ro 2-ga 366-1; burritos from ₩6500; ☺4.30pm-1am; 🛜; §Line 1 or 2 to City Hall, Exit 2)

Wangbijip   KOREAN $$

12 Map p52, D2

Head upstairs to this tasteful Korean restaurant popular for grilled meats and other traditional dishes such as *samgyetang* (ginseng chicken soup) and bibimbap. (왕비집; www.wangbijib. com; 2nd fl, 34-1 Myeongdong 1-ga, Jung-gu; mains from ₩12,000; ☺11.30am-11pm; §Line 4 to Myeongdong, Exit 8)

Potala   TIBETAN, INDIAN $$

13 Map p52, D2

Books about Tibet and colourful crafts and pictures adorn this restaurant where you can sample the cuisine of the high Himalaya plateau, including *momo* (dumplings) cooked by Nepali chefs. While not exclusively vegetarian, there are plenty of vegie options. (www. potala.co.kr; 4th fl, 32-14 Myeongdong 2-ga, Jung-gu; mains ₩9,000-20,000; ☺11am-11pm; ✐; §Line 4 to Myeongdong, Exit 8)

WILL ROBB/GETTY IMAGES ©

Namsangol Hanok Village (p54)

Soo:P Coffee Flower
CAFE $$

14 Map p52, C2

A slice of arty Hongdae in downtown Seoul, this earthy light-filled cafe is filled with pot plants and makes a great spot for a light meal such as gourmet sandwiches, organic vegie bibimbap and homemade cakes. It also does a good coffee. (www.soopcoffee flower.com; 97 Sogong-ro, Jung-gu; coffee ₩2500, sandwiches ₩8000; ⊙11am-10pm Mon-Sat; 🛜; 🅂 Line 1 or 2 to City Hall, Exit 7)

Gogung
KOREAN $$

15 Map p52, E2

An atmospheric restaurant that specialises in authentic Jeonju bibimbap, among other varieties, accompanied by live traditional Korean music. (고궁; www.gogung.co.kr; 37 Myeongdong 8ga-gil, Jung-gu; mains from ₩11,000; ⊙9am-10pm; 🛜 ✐; 🅂 Line 4 to Myeong-dong, Exit 10)

Chung-jeong-gak
ITALIAN $$

16 Map p52, A3

Housed in an attractive red-brick, Western-style building from around 1910 with white-wood wrap-around verandah, this restaurant is a fragment of Seoul's past. The Italian food is delicious, and as it's across from a branch of **Nanta Theatre** (✆02-739 8288; www.nanta.co.kr; 476 Chungjeongno 3-ga, Seodaemungu; tickets ₩40,000-60,000; ⊙shows 5pm & 8pm; 🅂 Line 5 to Chungjeongno,

Exit 7), it's a good spot for a pre- or postshow meal. Inside it also has an art gallery. From the subway exit turn right and it's on your right. (충정각; ☎02-313 0424; Chungjeong-ro, Seodaemungu; mains from ₩15,000, set menu from ₩22,000; ⊙11am-10pm Mon-Sat; 🛜; ⑤Line 2 or 5 to Chungjeongno, Exit 9)

Gosang KOREAN $$$

17 Map p52, D1

One worth dressing up for, this classy restaurant specialises in vegetarian temple dishes that date from the Goryeo dynsasty. It's all set-course, traditional-style banquets here, and there's also a meat option. It's in a posh food court in the basement of the Center 1 Building. (고상; ☎02-6030 8955; www.baru-gosang.com; 67 Suha-dong, Jung-gu; lunch/dinner set course ₩39,900/50,000; ⊙11.30am-3.30pm & 5.30-10pm; 🖋; ⑤Line 2 to Euljiro 1-ga, Exit 4)

N.Grill INTERNATIONAL $$$

18 Map p52, E5

Led by Michelin-starred British chef Duncan Robertson, this upmarket revolving restaurant sits uptop the iconic N Seoul Tower (p46). Views are amazing, as is its French-style cooking mixed with Korean influences. Reservations are essential. Downstairs, the open-air N Terrace is a good spot for a cocktail with a view. (☎02-3455 9297; www.nseoultower.co.kr; N Seoul Tower, Namsan; lunch/dinner from ₩55,000/95,000; ⊙11am-3pm & 5-11pm; ⑤Line 4 to Myeong-dong, Exit 3 then cable car)

Drinking

Craftworks MICROBREWERY

19 Map p52, F1

Hidden away in an underground mall in Seoul's downtown business district, this branch of Craftworks microbrew pub is a good spot to take a break with an excellent choice of craft beers. (www.craftworkstaphouse.com/downtown; Pine Avenue Mall, 100 Eulji-ro, Jung-gu; ⑤Line 2 or 3 to Euljiro 3-ga, Exit 12)

Caffe Themselves CAFE

20 Map p52, E1

A worthy stop for those who take their coffee seriously, here baristas know how to do a decent single-origin espresso, slow drip or cold brew. They roast their own beans, which they sell by the bag, as well as having ready-made samples to try. (www.caffethemselves.com; 388 Samil-daero, Jongno-gu; coffee ₩5500; ⊙10am-10pm; 🛜; ⑤Line 1 to Jonggak, Exit 12)

Walkabout BAR

21 Map p52, E3

Among Myeong-dong's backpacker enclave leading up to Namsan, this travel-themed bar is run by a couple of young travel nuts who serve Korean craft beers on tap. (http://blog.naver.com/walkaboutnu; 49 Toegye-ro 20-gil, Jung-gu; ⊙10am-midnight Mon-Sat, 2-10pm Sun; 🛜; ⑤Line 4 to Myeongdong, Exit 3)

Nanta performance

SEONG JOON CHO/GETTY IMAGES ©

Coffee Libre
CAFE

22 Map p52, E2

A tiny branch of this speciality coffee roaster with a somewhat bizarre location within the Myeong-dong Cathedral complex, but it makes for a good pit stop to refuel on single-origin pour overs, aeropress or espressos. (www.coffeelibre.kr; Myeong-dong Cathedral, 74 Myeong-dong-gil, Jung-gu; ⊘9am-9pm; ⓢLine 4 to Myeongdong, Exit 4)

Cat Cafe
CAFE

23 Map p52, D2

One of Seoul's growing legion of pet-themed cafes, here you sip a hot drink while cuddling a number of prized-looking cats. (www.godabang.

com; 6th fl, 51-14 Myeongdong 2-ga, Jung-gu; adult/child incl drink ₩8000/5000; ⊘1-10pm Mon-Fri, noon-10pm Sat & Sun; ⓢLine 4 to Myeongdong, Exit 6)

Entertainment

Nanta Theatre
PERFORMING ARTS

24 Map p52, D2

Running for more than 15 years, and with no end in sight, is Korea's most successful nonverbal performance – Nanta. Set in a kitchen, this high-octane, 90-minute show mixes magic tricks, *samulnori* folk music, drumming, kitchen utensils, comedy, dance, martial arts and audience participation. It's top-class entertainment that has been a hit wherever it plays. There's another venue in Chungjeongo (p59). (눈스퀘어; ☑02-739 8288; www.nanta.co.kr; 3rd fl, Unesco Bldg, 26 Myeongdong-gil, Jung-gu; tickets ₩40,000-60,000; ☺2pm, 5pm & 8pm; ⑤Line 4 to Myeongdong, Exit 6)

National Theater of Korea
THEATRE

 25 ⭐ Map p52, H5

The several venues here are home to the national drama, *changgeuk* (Korean opera), orchestra and dance

 Top Tip

Korea House

Scoring a hat trick for high-quality food, entertainment and shopping is **Korea House** (한국의집; Map p52, F3; ☑02-2266 9101; www.koreahouse. or.kr; 10 Toegye-ro 36-gil, Jung-gu; set menu lunch/dinner ₩45,000/68,200, performances ₩50,000; ☺lunch noon-2pm Mon-Fri, dinner 5-6.30pm & 7-8.30pm; performances 6.30pm & 8.30pm; shop 10am-8pm; ⑤Line 3 or 4 to Chungmuro, Exit 3). A dozen dainty, artistic courses make up the royal banquet. The *hanok* (traditional wooden home), the waitstaff clad in *hanbok* (traditional clothing), the *gayageum* (zither) music, and the platters and boxes the food is served in are all part of the experience. The intimate theatre stages two hour-long dance and music performances, which you can see independently of eating here.

companies. Free concerts and movies are put on in summer at the outdoor stage. Walk 10 minutes here or hop on bus 2 at the stop behind Exit 6 of the subway. (☑02-2280 4122; www.ntok. go.kr; 59 Jangchungdan-ro, Jung-gu; ⑤Line 3 Dongguk University, Exit 6)

Jeongdong Theater
THEATRE

26 ⭐ Map p52, A1

Most famous for its critically acclaimed musical *Miso*, this theatre company also produces a number of traditional nonverbal musicals. (☑02-751 1500; www.jeongdong.or.kr; 43 Jeongdong-gil, Jung-gu; tickets ₩30,000-40,000; ☺4pm & 8pm Tue-Sun; ⑤Line 1 or 2 to City Hall, Exit 2)

Shopping

Shinsegae
DEPARTMENT STORE

 27 🔒 Map p52, C3

Wrap yourself in luxury inside the Seoul equivalent of Harrods. It's split over two buildings, the older part based in a gorgeous 1930 colonial building that was Seoul's first department store Mitsukoshi. Check out local designer fashion labels and the opulent supermarket in the basement with a food court; another food court is up on the 11th floor of the building with an attached roof garden to relax in. (신세계백화점; ☑02-2026 9000; www.shinsegae.com; 63 Sogong-ro, Jung-gu; ☺10.30am-8pm; ⑤Line 4 to Hoehyeon, Exit 7)

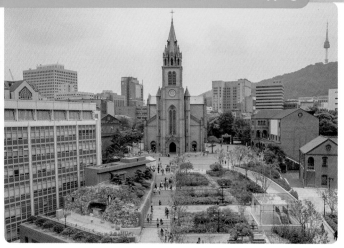

Myeong-dong Catholic Cathedral (p56)

Lotte Department Store
DEPARTMENT STORE

28 🔒 Map p52, D2

Retail behemoth Lotte spreads its tentacles across four buildings: the main department store, Lotte Young Plaza, Lotte Avenuel and a duty-free shop. Also here is a multiplex cinema, restaurants and hotel. (롯데백화점; 📞02-771 2500; http://store.lotteshopping.com; 81 Namdaemun-ro, Jung-gu; ⏲10.30am-8pm; Ⓢ Line 2 to Euljiro 1-ga, Exit 8)

Lab 5
FASHION

29 🔒 Map p52, D2

No need to root around Dongdaemun Market for the latest hot K-designers, with this store showcasing the designs of 100 rising stars including participants of *Project Runway Korea*. (Level 5, Noon Sq, Myeongdong 2-ga, Jung-gu; Ⓢ Line 2 to Euljiro 1-ga, Exit 6)

Åland
FASHION

30 🔒 Map p52, D2

Spread over three levels this multi-label boutique mixes up vintage and garage-sale items with new designer pieces to wear and decorate your home with. For menswear head to the building across the street. (www.a-land.co.kr; 30 Myeongdong 6-gil, Jung-gu; ⏲10.30am-10.30pm; Ⓢ Line 4 to Myeong-dong, Exit 6)

Explore

Hongdae & Around

Seoul's principal student quarter comprises Hongdae, Edae and Sinchon. These are youthful, creative districts short on traditional sights, and big on modern-day diversions and entertainment. South of Hongdae across the Han River, the island of Yeouido has several places of interest, all easily visited if you hire a bike in its riverside or central park.

The Sights in a Day

Spend the first half of the day sightseeing south of Hongdae, starting with **Jeoldusan Martyrs' Shrine** (p70). Then grab a bike to cycle along the Han River, stopping at **Seonyudo Park** (p72) and the **World Cup Park** (p71). Check out the views from atop **63 City** (p72) and push on to **Noryangjin Fish Market** (p73) for a seafood lunch.

Head into hip Hongdae to explore its arty streets, boutique stores and cool cafes, including **Anthracite** (p75). If you're around on a Saturday, don't miss the **Free Market** (p78), which has craft stalls and entertainers. Pop by **KT&G Sangsang-Madang** (p67) to see what's showing.

Start the evening digging into Korean pancakes and a bottle of quality *makgeolli* (milky rice wine) from **Wolhyang** (p75). Then check out the local bands that take your fancy at venues such as **DGBD** (p67). If nothing's to your liking, there are plenty of bars, offering everything from craft beer at **Magpie** (p67) to clubbing at **M2** (p77).

For a local's day in Hipster Hongdae, see p66.

Local Life

Best of Seoul

Getting There

S **Subway** Line 2, 4 or A'REX train to Hongik University; Line 6 to Hapjeong; Line 5 or 9 to Yeouido

Local Life
Hipster Hongdae

Centred on Hongkik University, Hongdae is where the cool kids hang out. Home to Korea's leading art and design institution, it's a fertile patch for chaotic creativity and unbridled hedonism. As well as bars, galleries and street art, it's also the epicentre for the K-Indie scene, with scores of live-music clubs and dance spots.

1 Shopping for Art

Representing local artists and craftspeople, several of whom also sell their goods at the Free Market on Saturday, **Key** (www.welcomekey. net; 48-5 Wausan-ro 29-gil; ⊘noon-10pm Tue-Sun; ⑤Line 2 to Hongik University, Exit 8) is a small gallery and showroom that offers affordable, exclusive items, from jewellery to pottery, to fabric art and paintings.

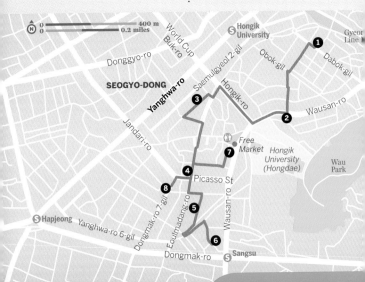

❷ Recycled Boutiques

Ecofriendly shoes, bags and other goods – some made from recycled products – are sold at **Little Farmers** (www.littlefarmers.co.kr; 112 Wausan-ro; ⏱11.30am-8.30pm; Ⓢ Line 2 to Hongik University, Exit 8), an attractive basement store. Look for the wallets and bags made from recycled newspapers and magazines. You'll also find a few K-Indie CDs here and other colourful accessories.

❸ Grab a Bite

On a street with several other atmospheric Japanese restaurants, **Menya Sandaime** (☎02-332 4129; www.menyasandaime.com; 24 Hongik-ro 3-gil; mains ₩7000-9000; ⏱noon-10pm; Ⓢ Line 2 to Hongik University, Exit 9) ramen shop is the real deal. It's a great place for single diners, who can sit at the counter by the open kitchen watching the hip, tattooed chefs carefully craft bowls of delicious noodles.

❹ Local Art Scene

The visually striking **KT&G Sangsang-Madang** (KT&G 상상마당; ☎02-330 6200; www.sangsangmadang.com; 65 Eoulmadang-ro; ⏱shop noon-11pm, gallery 1-10pm; Ⓢ Line 2 to Hongik University, Exit 5) is home to an art-house cinema, a concert space (hosting top indie bands) and galleries that focus on experimental, fringe exhibitions. There's also a great design shop for gifts on the ground floor.

❺ Coffee & Vintage Furniture

Soaring ceilings and space, filled with designer and retro furniture, sets **aA Café** (www.aadesignmuseum.com; 19-18 Wausan-ro 17-gil; ⏱cafe noon-midnight, shop to 8pm; 📶; Ⓢ Line 6 to Sangsu, Exit 1) apart. It's a great place to hang out with a coffee, before heading down to the basement to browse classic furniture pieces in the shop-museum.

❻ Stop in for Ice Cream

A sweet diversion in Hongdae, **Fell & Cole** (www.fellncole.com; 39-21 Wausan-ro; 1 scoop ₩4200; ⏱noon-10pm; Ⓢ Line 6 to Sangsu, Exit 1) offers fabulous ice cream and sorbet. The flavours change all the time, but might include perilla leaf, parsley lemonade, burnt banana and *kalimotxo* (aka Jesus Juice).

❼ Craft Beer

You don't need to be in Itaewon to drink craft beer, with **Magpie** (www.magpiebrewing.com; 6-15 Wausan-ro 19-gil; ⏱5pm-2am Tue-Thu, 5pm-3am Fri, 2pm-3am Sat, 2pm-2am Sun; Ⓢ Line 2 to Hongik University, Exit 9) microbrewery now in Hongdae offering a range of its fine ales.

❽ Local Music Scene

First-generation K-Indie bands such as Crying Nut came into the spotlight at **DGBD** (디지비디; ☎02-322 3792; http://cafe.daum.net/dgbd; 23 Jandari-ro; admission ₩10,000; ⏱8-11pm; Ⓢ Line 2 or 6 or Hapjeong, Exit 3), Hongdae's legendary live-music venue. It's standing room only and there's a balcony.

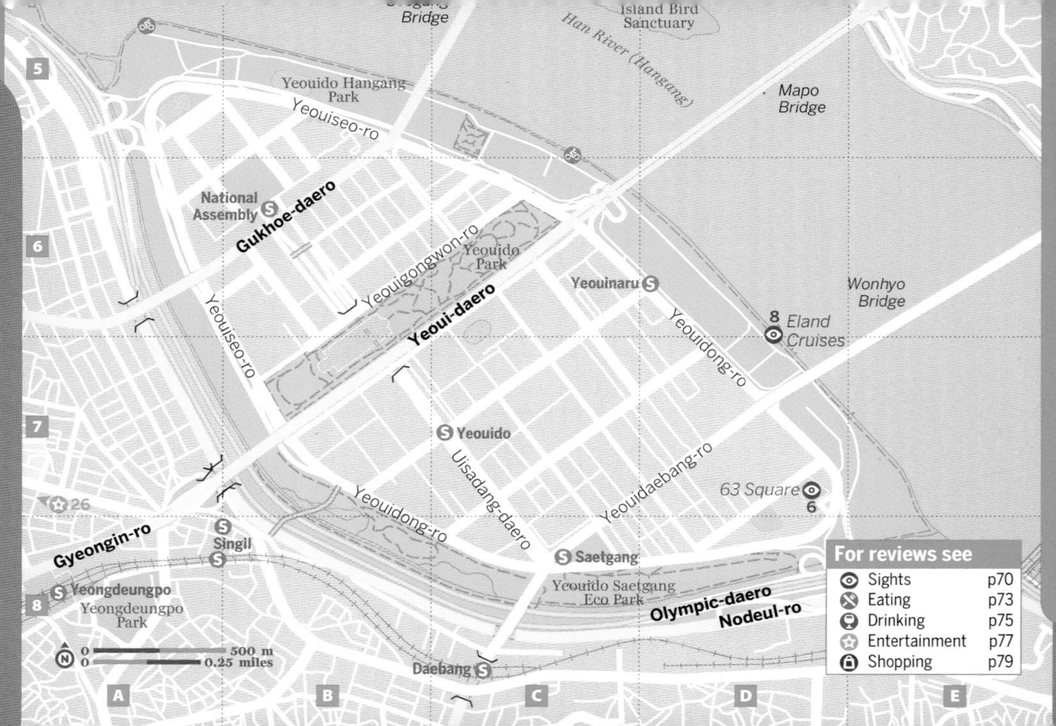

Wonhyo Bridge

Mapo Bridge

Island Bird Sanctuary

Han River (Hangang)

Bridge

8 Eland Cruises

Yeouidong-ro

63 Square

Yeouidaebang-ro

Nodeul-ro

Olympic-daero

Yeouinaru Ⓢ

Saetgang Ⓢ

Yeouido Saetgang Eco Park

Yeouido

Uisadang-daero

Yeouido Park

Yeouigongwon-ro

Yeoui-daero

Yeouidong-ro

Daebang Ⓢ

Yeouido Hangang Park

Yeouiseo-ro

Gukhoe-daero

National Assembly Ⓢ

Yeouiseo-ro

Singil Ⓢ

Yeongdeungpo Park

Gyeongin-ro

Yeongdeungpo Ⓢ

500 m
0.25 miles

Sights

Jeoldusan Martyrs' Shrine   MUSEUM

1 ◎ Map p68, A3

Jeoldusan means 'Beheading Hill' – this is where up to 2000 Korean Catholics were executed in 1866 following a royal decree, most thrown off the high cliff here into the Han River. Next to the chapel (where Mass is held daily at 10am and 3pm) the museum includes some of grizzly wooden torture equipment used on the Catholic

Local Life
Mullae Arts Village

Artists and designers have started to move in beside the steel workers and welders in the light-industrial area of Mullae-dong, rebranded as **Mullae Arts Village** (문래예술촌; Mullae-dong, Yoengdeungpo-gu; Ⓢ Line 2 to Mullae, Exit 7). On the main road you'll find **Chichipopo Library** (☎ 02-2068 1667; www.facebook.com/chichipopolibrary; 428-1 Dorim-ro, Yeongdeungpo-gu; ⏰ 10am-11.30pm Mon-Fri, 11am-11pm Sat & Sun; 🛜; Ⓢ Line 2 to Mullae, Exit 7), a relaxing self-serve cafe and gallery space with mismatched furniture, cheap Western-style eats and drinks, and a rooftop garden. Also, look up what's happening at **Seoul Arts Space – Mullae** (☎ 02-2676 4300; http://english.sfac.or.kr; 5-4 Gyeongin-ro 88-gil, Yeongdeungpo-gu; Ⓢ Line 2 to Mullae, Exit 7), which includes a studio theatre and gallery.

martyrs, 27 of whom have been made saints. There are also books, diaries and relics of the Catholic converts. (절두산 순교성지; ☎ 02-3142 4434; www.jeoldusan.or.kr; 6 Tojeong-ro; museum by donation; ⏰ shrine 24hr, museum 9.30am-5pm Tue-Sun; Ⓢ Line 2 or 6 to Hapjeong, Exit 7)

Ewha Womans University   ARCHITECTURE, MUSEUM

2 ◎ Map p68, E1

Come to this venerable university, founded in 1886 by American Methodist missionary Mary Scranton, to view Dominque Perrault's stunning main entrance, a building that dives six storeys underground and is split by a broad cascade of steps leading up to the Gothic-style 1935 Pfeiffer Hall. Walking through here feels like going through the parting of the Red Sea. (www.ewha.ac.kr; Ewhayeodae-gil, Seodaemun-gu; Ⓢ Line 2 to Ewha Womans University, Exit 2)

War & Women's Human Rights Museum   MUSEUM

3 ◎ Map p68, B1

In Korea the survivors of sexual slavery by the Japanese military during WWII (know euphemistically as 'comfort women') are respectfully called *halmoni* (grandmother). When you enter this well-designed and powerfully moving museum you'll be given a card printed with the story of a *halmoni* helping you to connect with the tragic history of these women. (전쟁과여성인권박물관; ☎ 02-365 4016; www.womenandwar.net; 20 World Cup Buk-ro 11-gil,

Ewha Womans University

Mapo-gu; adult/child under 14yr/youth 14-19yr ₩3000/1000/2000; ⊙1-6pm Tue, Thu-Sat, 3-6pm Wed; Ⓢ Line 2 to Hongik University, Exit 1, then 🚍6, 15, 7711, 7011, 7016 or 7737)

Modern Design Museum   MUSEUM

4 ◎ Map p68, C2

The items displayed on the two floors of this small museum trace the history of modern design in Korea from the 1880s to contemporary times. Not much is labelled in English but it's still a fascinating collection that spans a wide range of products from 19th-century books and newspapers to 1960s toys and electronics and posters for the 1988 Olympics. (근현대 디자인박물관; www.designmuseum.or.kr; 36 Wausan-ro 30-gil, Mapo-gu; adult/child ₩5000/4000; ⊙10am-6pm Tue-Sun; Ⓢ Line 2 to Hongik University, Exit 9)

World Cup Park   PARK

5 ◎ Map p68, A1

These five connected parks (Pyeong-hwa, Nanjicheon, Nanji Hangang, Haneul Park and Noeul) were created for the 2002 FIFA World Cup out of former landfill and waste ground. Today the area is one of Seoul's largest green spaces threaded through with cycle and walking paths, sporting facilities, and leafy relaxation spots. Climb hilly Haneul Park for great views across the area. (월드컵공원; http://worldcuppark.seoul.go.kr; 251 World Cup-ro, Mapo-gu; Ⓢ Line 6 to World Cup Stadium, Exit 1)

ARTZENTER/SHUTTERSTOCK ©

Top Tip

Bicycle Hire

Cycling the 15km route around Yeouido and along the Han River is a pleasant activity. Walk east from the subway exit towards the Hangang Cruise Terminal in Yeouido Hangang Park to find a **bicycle rental stall** (Map p68, C6; 1st hr ₩3000, every extra 15mins ₩500; ⏰9am-5pm); bring some form of photo ID to leave as a deposit.

MARTIN RICHARDSON © ROUGH GUIDES/GETTY IMAGES ©

Skyscraper, 63 Square

63 Square
VIEWPOINT

6 ⊙ Map p68, D7

From the basement of the gold-tinted glass skyscraper, one of Seoul's tallest buildings, you can access five different attractions, the pick of which is **63 Sky Art Gallery** (adult/child under 14yr/youth 14-19yr ₩13,000/11,000/12,000; ⏰10am-10pm). This combines a 60th-floor observation deck offering panoramic views, with top-class, regularly changing art exhibitions. (☎02-789 5663; www.63.co.kr; 50, 63-ro, Yeongdeungpo-gu; ⑤Line 5 to Yeouinaru, Exit 4)

Seonyudo Park
PARK

7 ⊙ Map p68, A3

A former water-filtration plant on an island in the Han River has been transformed into this award-winning park. The old industrial buildings have been cleverly adapted as part of the new landscaping and gardens which include lily-covered ponds, plant nurseries and exhibitions halls. Either walk here from the subway station or cycle from Yeouido. (http://hangang.seoul.go.kr; admission free; ⏰6am-midnight; ⑤Line 9 to Seonyudo, Exit 2)

Eland Cruises
CRUISE

8 ⊙ Map p68, D6

A variety of day and night short sightseeing cruises depart from this Yeouido pier, one of three that the company's boats pause at along the Han River. (www.elandcruise.com; Han River

Park, Yeouido; cruises from ₩12,000; ⊘11am-8.40pm; §Line 5 to Yeouinaru, Exit 3)

Eating

Tuk Tuk Noodle Thai   THAI $

 Map p68, C1

Credited with kicking off a trend for more authentic Thai restaurants in Seoul, Tuk Tuk is a jauntily decorated basement space close by Dongjin Market. Thai chefs whack out a broad menu of spicy dishes that don't compromise on flavour. (☑070-4407 5130; blog.naver.com/tuktuknoodle; 37 Yeonhui-ro; mains ₩7500-12,000; ⊘noon-3pm & 5-10.30pm; §Line 2 to Hongik University, Exit 3)

Slobbie   KOREAN $$

 Map p68, B2

Simple, tasty dishes such as bibimbap and *jjigae* (stews) are served in pleasant, modern surroundings at this admirable social enterprise training young chefs from challenged backgrounds and providing jobs for single mothers. The restaurant name is pronounced 'Slow-bee', indicating its aim to promote a slower, healthier and more organic lifestyle for Seoulites. (☑02-3143 5525; www.facebook.com/slobbie8; 5th fl, 10 Hongik-ro 6-gil, Mapo-gu; meals ₩8000; ⊘11.30am-11.30pm Mon-Sat; ⛊; §Line 2 to Hongik University, Exit 9)

Seonyudo Park

 Local Life

Noryangjin Fish Market

Providing terrific photo opportunities, **Noryangjin Fish Market** (노량진수산시장; Map p68, D8; www.susansijang.co.kr; 688 Nodeul-ro, Dongjak-gu; ⊘24hr; §Line 1 to Noryangjin, Exit 1) supplies every kind of aquatic lifeform to restaurants, fish shops and the general public. If you want to view the market at its liveliest, get here for the auctions, which kick off around 1am. Otherwise, come around meal times and buy seafood and then get it cooked (starting from ₩5000, depending on what you have) at one of the restaurants within the market.

Loving Hut

VEGAN $

11 Map p68, D1

A variety of slogans in English urge diners on to a more compassionate, meat-free life at this pastel-shaded, pleasantly modern cafe. It serves very tasty and good-value Korean meals with rice, noodles, vegies – and no animal products. (www.lovinghut.com; 35 Yonsei-ro, Seodaemun-gu; mains ₩5000-6000; ⏱11.30am-3.30pm & 4.30-9pm Mon-Fri, 11.30am-9pm Sat & Sun; 🛜🍴; Ⓢ Line 2 to Sinchon, Exit 2)

Ciuri Ciuri

ITALIAN $$

12 Map p68, B3

Run by Italian couple Enrico and Fiore, the tasty and unusual – for Seoul – specialities here hail from Sicily, such as *arancine* (saffron-flavoured risotto balls), *anelletti* (small ring pasta) and a special type of sausage. The place is decorated as if you're on holiday in Sicily itself with staw-hat lampshades and colourfully painted tiled tables and water bottles. (🛜02-749 9996; www.ciuriciuri.co.kr; 2nd fl, 314-3 Sangsu-dong, Mapo-gu; mains ₩7000-18,000; ⏱noon-3pm & 6-11pm Mon-Fri, noon-11pm Sat & Sun; Ⓢ Line 6 to Sangsu, Exit 1)

Taverna de Portugal

PORTUGUESE $$

13 Map p68, C3

Porto-native Augusto and his Korean wife Heera have made their mark in Hongdae serving up authentically spicy and very moreish piri-piri grilled whole chicken or the Fracesinha, a chunky sandwich of pork and sausage smothered in melted cheese and dowsed with a tomato-and-beer sauce. Their set menus (₩26,000) are big enough for two to share. (🛜02-3144 4189; 9 Wausan-ro 13-gil Mapo-gu; mains from ₩14,000; ⏱noon-3.30pm & 5-10pm Wed & Thu, noon-10pm Fri-Sun; Ⓢ Line 6 to Sangsu, Exit 1)

63 Buffet Pavilion

BUFFET $$$

With too many temptations to count, this gourmet buffet (see 6 ⏱ Map p68, D7) is a good way to sample a range of Asian and other cuisines. Children up to 18 eat for about half price. (🛜02-789 5731; www.63buffet.co.kr; 63 City, 50, 63-ro, Yeongdeungpo-gu; lunch Mon-Fri ₩65,000, dinner ₩78,000; ⏱noon-3pm & 6-10pm Mon-Fri, 11am-3.30pm & 5-10pm Sat & Sun; Ⓢ Line 5 to Yeouinaru, Exit 4)

Local Life

Dongjin Market

While the **Dongjin Market** (Map p68, C1; www.facebook.com/makedongjin; 198 Seongmisan-ro, Mapo-gu; ⏱1-6pm Sat; Ⓢ Line 2 to Hongik University, Exit 3) only opens on Saturdays, the rest of the week bars and cafes stay open in and around the market, such as the Mexican joint **B'Mucho**, gourmet coffee roasters **Cafe Libre** and Vietnamese *banh-mi* (bread roll) stall **Lie Lie Lie**.

SEONG JOON CHO/GETTY IMAGES ©

Noryangjin Fish Market (p73)

Drinking

Anthracite CAFE

14 🚇 Map p68, B3

An old shoe factory is the location for one of Seoul's top independent coffee-roaster and cafe operations. Drinks are made using the hand-drip method at a counter made out of an old conveyor belt. Upstairs is a spacious lounge and there's outdoor seating on the roof. (www.anthracitecoffee.com; 10 Tojeong-ro 5-gil; ⊗11am-midnight; 🛜; 🚇 Line 6 to Sangsu, Exit 4)

Wolhyang BAR

15 🚇 Map p68, C2

Specialising in *makgeolli* (milky rice wine) from around Korea and other local liquors, this brightly decorated, spacious 2nd-floor bar is a great place to sample traditional alcoholic drinks. It also has various fruity and nutty flavours of *makgeolli* as well as decent food such as savoury pancakes. (📞02-332 9202; www.tasteofthemoon.com; 27 Wausan-ro 29-gil, Mapo-gu; ⊗11.30pm-2am Mon-Sat, to 1am Sun; 🛜; 🚇 Line 2 to Hongik University, Exit 8)

Café Sukkara

CAFE, BAR

16 Map p68, C2

There's a fantastic range of drinks and some very tasty things to eat (try the butter-chicken curry) at this shabby-chic, farmhouse-style cafe with a contemporary Japanese flair. They make their own juices and liquors – try the black shandy gaff, a mix of homemade ginger ale and Magpie Brewery dark beer. (✒02-334 5919; www.sukkara.co.kr; Sanullim Bldg, 327-9 Seogyo-dong, Mapo-gu; ☺11am-midnight Tue-Sun; ☎; ⑤Line 2 to Hongik University, Exit 9)

Local Life
Hongdae's Animal Cafes

For the price of a drink, you can have quality time with a variety of cuddlesome creatures at theme cafes around Hongdae: **Thanks Nature Cafe** (Map p68, C2; ✒02-335 7470; www.facebook.com/TNcafe; 121 Prugio Bldg, 10 Hongik-ro, Mapo-gu; ☺11am-10pm; ⑤Line 2 to Hongik University, Exit 9) has a couple of cute sheep that live in the enclosure outside; **Bau House** (Map p68, B3; ✒070-7550 5153; www.baumall.co.kr; 64 Yanghwa-ro, Mapo-gu; ☺1.30-11pm Mon-Sat, 12.30-11pm Sun; ⑤Line 2 or 6 to Hapjeong, Exit 3) has pedigree pooches to play with; while **TableA** (Map p68, C2; www.table-a.co.kr; 146 Wausan-ro, Mapo-gu; ☺8am-1am; ⑤Line 2 to Hongik University, Exit 7) is the place for cats, including kittens.

Keg B

PUB

17 Map p68, B3

This cosy craft beer pub on the top floor of a small backstreet block is a good place to savour a pint or two. Choose between four local beers on tap and scores of bottled ales from around the world, served alongside snacks such as pizza, fried chicken and nachos. (✒02-334 1979; 19 Wausan-ro 13-gil, Mapo-gu; ☺5pm-midnight; ⑤Line 6 to Sangsu, Exit 1)

Yri Cafe

CAFE

18 Map p68, B3

Browse local and imported books and magazines on art and design at this convivial boho hang-out that works just as well as a daytime cafe as it does a night-time drinks venue. (http://cafe.naver.com/yricafe; 27 Wausan-ro 3-gil, Mapo-gu; ☺11am-1am Mon-Fri, to 2am Sat & Sun; ⑤Line 6 to Sangsu, Exit 4)

Labris

LESBIAN, BAR

19 Map p68, C2

On the 8th floor of the same building as On the Spot boutique, this is a comfortable women-only space that's lesbian-oriented but not exclusively so. DJ nights are Friday to Sunday when the minimum charge for a drink and compulsory *anju* (bar snacks) is ₩15,000. (라브리스; ✒02-333 5276; 81-Wausan-ro, Mapo-gu; ☺7pm-2am Mon-Thu, to 5am Fri-Sun; ⑤Line 6 to Sangsu, Exit 1)

Understand
K-Indie

Hongdae is the home of Seoul's K-Indie scene, with divey venues catering to bands. The scene has flourished over the past few years, with many bands receiving international recognition. Some to watch out for include Jambinai, a postrock band who combine traditional instruments with heavy guitar riffs; alt-indie bands the Dead Buttons or the Koxx; the Patients and Yellow Monsters for punk rock; and electronica act, Idiotape. Refer to **Korea Gig Guide** (www.koreagigguide.com) for a listing of bands.

M2

CLUB

20 Map p68, B2

Deep underground is M2, one of the largest and best Hongdae clubs. It has a high ceiling and plenty of lights and visuals. Top local and international DJs spin mainly progressive house music. (☑02-3143 7573; www.ohoo.net/m2; 20-5 Jandari-ro; Sun-Thu ₩10,000, Fri & Sat ₩20,000; ⏰9.30pm-4.30am Sun-Thu, 8.30pm-6.30am Fri & Sat; 🚇Line 6 to Sangsu, Exit 1)

Club MWG

CLUB

21 Map p68, B2

Myoung Wol Gwan (MWG) translates as 'bight moon house' but lunar sightings are not on the agenda from this dark, basement venue, one of Hongdae's longest-running clubs. Come here for the GLBT-friendly **Meet Market** (www.facebook.com/meetmarket seoul) queer party events as well as indie bands and DJ nights. (www.facebook.com/clubmwg1; 6-5, Wausan-ro 19-gil, Mapo-gu; ⏰10pm-5am Fri & Sat; 🚇Line 2 to Hongik University, Exit 2)

Entertainment

Mudaeruk

LIVE MUSIC

22 ⭐ Map p68, B3

The 'Lost Continent of Mu' has been hiding out in Sangsu-dong all these years? Join in-the-know hipsters for shows by bands and DJs specialising in electronic music in the basement on weekends. Upstairs is a stylish cafe-bar with craft beer, sharing boards of food and great fish and chips. (무대륙; ☑02-332 8333; www.mudaeruk.com; 12 Tojeong-ro 5-gil; admission from ₩10,000; 🛜; 🚇Line 6 to Sangsu, Exit 4)

Club Evans

JAZZ

23 ⭐ Map p68, C3

Appealing across the generations, Evans offers top-grade jazz and a great atmosphere. Get here early if you want a seat or book ahead. It releases its own label CDs, too. Monday is jam night. (☑02-337 8361; www.clubevans.com; 63-Wausan-ro, Mapo-gu; admission ₩10,000; ⏰7.30pm-midnight Sun-Thu, to 2am Fri & Sat; 🚇Line 6 to Sangsu, Exit 1)

FF

LIVE MUSIC

24 ⭐ Map p68, B2

A top live venue with up to eight local indie bands playing at the weekend until midnight. Afterwards it becomes a dance club with DJs. (☏011-9025 3407; www.facebook.com/pages/Club-FF/ 213154478733706; Hongdae; admission ₩10,000; ◷7pm-6am; ⑤Line 6 to Sangsu, Exit 1)

Café BBang

LIVE MUSIC

25 ⭐ Map p68, C2

You're sure to catch something interesting here – apart from gigs by indie artists and bands, it also hosts film screenings, art exhibitions and parties. (카페 빵; http://cafe.daum.net/cafebbang; 12 Wausan-ro 29-gil, Mapo-gu; ◷7pm-6am; ⑤Line 2 to Hongik University, Exit 8)

Club Ta

LIVE MUSIC

The hub of Hongdae's ska and ska-punk scene, sets at Ta (see 24 ⭐ Map p68, B2) usually run from around 9.30pm until midnight Friday to Sunday. It's bit more comfortable than your average Hongdae live-gig house. (☏02-6085 5150; www.facebook.com/theliveclubta; 10 Wausan-ro 17-gil, Mapo-gu; admission from ₩15,000; ◷7pm-3am Tue-Thu, to 5am Fri-Sun; ⑤Line 6 to Sangsu, Exit 1)

Indie Art-Hall GONG

PERFORMING ARTS

26 ⭐ Map p68, A7

Marked by a huge brick chimney, this still-operating steel-product factory has a large space on its 2nd floor devoted to a wide range of arts. Expect everything from visual- and performance-art shows to live gigs by K-Indie rockers. There's a shop selling some art and a cafe too. It's a couple of subway stations or a short taxi hop from Mullae. (☏02-2632 8848; www.gongcraft.net; 30 Seonyuseo-ro 30-gil, Yeongdeungpo-gu; ⚟; ⑤Line 5 to Yangpyeong, Exit 2)

Cinemateque KOFA

CINEMA

27 ⭐ Map p68, D1

Free classic and contemporary Korean films are on the bill at one of the three cinemas in this home of the

Top Tip

Saturday Markets

Aim to visit Hongdae on a Saturday for its lively weekly markets. Going strong since 2002, **Free Market** (Map p68, C2; www.freemarket. or.kr; Hongik University Playground, 19-3 Wausan-ro 21-gil, Mapo-gu; ◷1-6pm Sat Mar-Nov; ⑤Line 2 to Hongik University, Exit 9) is a great opportunity to meet the craftspeople and buy a unique souvenir, and has a good line-up of singers and bands who play all afternoon. Inside an old market arcade, **Dongjin Market** (p74) is a hotspot for browsers in hip Yeonnam-dong. Secondhand clothing, homemade jams and cookies and various crafts can be picked up here among other things.

PONTINO/ALAMY ©

Jeoldusan Martyrs' Shrine (p70)

Korean Film Archive. See the website for directions from the subway exit. (한국영상자료원; ☏02-3153 2001; www.koreafilm.org; 400 World Cup buk-ro, Mapo-gu; admission free; Ⓢ Line 6 to Susaek, Exit 2)

Shopping

Object Recycle ACCESSORIES

28 🔒 Map p68, C2

Although there's a bigger branch of Object in Hongdae, this one is notable for specialising in products that involve some element of re- or up-cycling, such as jeans and shirts made into bags, clocks from LP records and sidetables from cardboard boxes. (www.insideobject.com; 110 Wausan-ro, Mapo-gu; ◷11am-10pm; Ⓢ Line 2 to Hongik University, Exit 9)

Gentle Monster ACCESSORIES

29 🔒 Map p68, B2

Sunglasses at night is *the* Hongdae look and this hip shop is the place to pick up the edgiest of shades and frames as worn by K-Popsters and TV stars. Imaginative and fun art installations change roughly every 25 days on the ground floor. (www.gentlemonster.com; 48 Dongmak-ro 7-gil, Mapo-gu; Ⓢ Line 2 or 6 to Hapjeong, Exit 3)

Explore

Itaewon & Around

Ever since the US army base was established here after WWII, Itaewon and the surrounding neighbourhoods have been defined by their international make-up. It's popular with young Koreans and expats, who can shop and relax in a multicultural mix of restaurants, bars and clubs. Besides having grown into one of Seoul's hippest hang-outs, Itaewon is also host to some of the city's premier museums and galleries.

The Sights in a Day

☀ There's a lot to see in one day, so get started with a big Western breakfast at **Suji's** (p91), before jumping on the subway to the **National Museum of Korea** (p82). Take a free 'best of' tour that covers the masterpieces, then stroll through its beautiful gardens. Pack a picnic to enjoy lunch.

☀ Take the subway to the **War Memorial of Korea** (p88) to learn about the catastrophic conflict that split Korea in half; aim to visit on a Friday for the 2pm military performance. After a few hours here, zip off to **Leeum Samsung Museum of Art** (p88) for world-class contemporary art.

☾ Take a much needed break, and grab dinner at one of Itaewon's many international restaurants, such as **Linus' BBQ** (p89). Then it's time to check out 'craft beer valley' where **Craftworks** (p85), among other microbreweries, has set up. Keep the party going at one of Itaewon's lively clubs; **Cakeshop** (p85) is one of the best.

For a local's evening in Itaewon, see p84.

 Top Sights

National Museum of Korea (p82)

Local Life

Bar Hopping in HBC (p84)

Best of Seoul

Eating
Vatos (p88)
Linus' BBQ (p89)

Drinking
Craftworks Taphouse (p85)
Damotori (p84)
Southside Parlor (p85)

Getting There

S **Subway** Line 6 to Itaewon, Noksapyeong or Hangangjin

Top Sights
National Museum of Korea

Korea's National Museum occupies a grand, marble-lined, modernist complex, built on the former golf course of the adjacent US military base. Set in landscaped parklands, the massive Great Hall displays a fraction of the museum's 270,000 cultural treasures from prehistoric times to the Joseon dynasty.

국립중앙박물관

◉ Map p86, D5

www.museum.go.kr

137 Seobinggo-ro

admission free

🕑 9am-6pm Tue, Thu & Fri, to 9pm Wed & Sat, to 7pm Sun

Ⓢ Line 1 or 4 to Ichon, Exit 2

Don't Miss

Exhibits

Among the must-see exhibits are the Baekje Incense Burner, a decorative metal piece that's an extraordinary example of the artistry of the 6th- to 7th-century Baekje kingdom; and the Golden Treasures from the Great Tomb of Hwangham, a delicate 5th-century gold belt and crown dripping with jade gems. In the 3rd-floor sculpture and craft galleries search out the Pensive Bodhisattva from the 7th century and beautiful examples of pottery. Also, look down on the top of the Goryeo dynasty Ten-Storey Pagoda carved from marble.

Gardens

The lovely surrounding park is best appreciated in clear weather, when the Great Hall is perfectly reflected in the large Reflecting Pond. The original Bosingak Bell is in the grounds near the picturesque Dragon Falls.

Other Museums

Outside is the Special Exhibition Hall, which hosts blockbuster international shows on anything from Pompeii to the Silk Road. Those interested in Korean language can visit the National Hangeul Museum, which provides an overview of its relatively recent history. Kids don't miss out either with the Children's Museum offering a snapshot of Korean culture with plenty of hands-on features and play spaces.

☑ Top Tips

▶ Hour-long English-language tours leave from the National Museum of Korea Great Hall lobby at 10am, 11am and 2pm Tuesday to Friday, and 11am and 2pm on weekends; alternatively you can rent an audioguide.

▶ The size of the museum is overwhelming, and it would take days to see it properly, so it's worth making several visits.

✗ Take a Break

There are a few restaurants in the complex, but if the weather is nice, you can picnic in the lovely gardens. A convenience store is near the main entrance, or come prepared with freshly baked goods from Itaewon's many bakeries.

Local Life
Bar Hopping in HBC

Itaewon is one of Seoul's hippest nightlife spots. It's packed with bars, pubs and clubs catering to those of all persuasions. The following places are in Haebangchon (HBC), an up-and-coming neighbourhood, and all specialise in quality alcohol: from traditional Korean liquors, to handcrafted ales and artisan cocktails.

....

1 Makgeolli at Damotori

A locals' favourite, the dimly lit **Damotori** (다모토리; 31 Sinheung-ro, Haebang-chon; ⏰6pm-1am Sun-Thu, to 2am Fri & Sat; 🛜; 🚇 Line 6 to Noksapyeong, Exit 2) specialises in quality *makgeolli* (milky rice wine), handpicked from around the country. As the first stop, it's also a good place to line the stomach, with delicious golden fried *haemulpajeon* (seafood pancake).

❷ Gin Time

An inspired mix of florist meets gin-bar, the perfumed scents at **Flower Gin** (250 Noksapyeong-daero; ⊘2pm-midnight Mon, Wed & Thu, from noon Fri-Sun; Ⓢ Line 6 to Noksapyeong, Exit 2) match the drinks superbly. This tiny bar only does gin-based drinks using Hendricks, and all come infused with a slice of cucumber and freshly plucked flower.

❸ Craft Beer at Magpie

A big player in Seoul's craft beer movement, **Magpie Brewing Co** (www.magpiebrewing.com; Noksapyeongro 54gil 7; ⊘3pm-1am; Ⓢ Line 6 to Noksapyeong, Exit 2) is split into two parts. Downstairs is Magpie Basement, a beer bunker with low-lying lamps, which serves pizaa (from ₩9000) and has eight beers on tap. Upstairs is the more intimate Brew Shop, which does occasional home-brew classes and tastings for ₩60,000.

❹ Booth

The original **Booth** (www.theboothpub.com; Itaewon-dong 705; ⊘noon-1am; Ⓢ Line 6 to Noksapyeong, Exit 2) brew pub has pop-art murals on its walls, and is known for its flagship Bill's pale ale and pepperoni pizza by the slice. There's also a divey industrial Booth Mansion branch near Itaewon station.

❺ Craftworks Taphouse

The original brewer to kick off Noksa-pyeong's craft beer scene, **Craftworks** (craftworkstaphouse.com; 651 Itaewon 2-dong; ⊘11am-midnight Mon-Fri, to 2am Sat & Sun; Ⓢ Line 6 to Noksapyeong, Exit 2) has secured a treasured place in the heart of Seoul's ale lovers. Order the paddle to sample its seven beers (₩10,500) and then decide which one to savour in a pint. It also features guest breweries, house wine and a quality menu of pub grub. Happy hour is 4pm to 6pm.

❻ Made in Pong Dang

In a scene dominated by North Americans, **Pong Dang** (www.pongdangsplash.com; 222-1 Noksapyeong; ⊘4pm-midnight Sun-Thu, 2pm-2am Fri & Sat; Ⓢ Line 6 to Noksapyeong, Exit 2) is an all-Korean affair, producing six of its beers on taps pulled from the wood-panelled bar, including pale ale, Belgian Blonde ale and seasonals such as oatmeal stout.

❼ Cocktails at Southside Parlor

From its roots as a food truck in Texas, the cocktail bar **Southside Parlor** (www.facebook.com/SouthsideParlor; 218 Noksapyeong-daero; ⊘6pm-midnight; Ⓢ Line 6 to Noksapyeong, Exit 2) is now in Itaewon. Here mixologists know their stuff, concocting labour-intensive originals and classics, served at an old-school copper bar counter. If you're hungry, it's got a quality menu of pulled-pork sandwiches, burgers etc. If the weather is nice, check out the Astroturf rooftop.

❽ Clubbing at Cakeshop

If you're still standing, head underground to **Cakeshop** (www.cakeshopseoul.com; 134 Itaewon-ro; entry incl 1 drink ₩20,000; ⊘Tue-Sat 10pm-5am; Ⓢ Line 6 to Noksapyeong, Exit 2), Itaewon's hippest club for electronic beats spun by international and top local DJs. It attracts a lively, mixed crowd. Expect long queues.

A B C D

N 0 ——————————— 500 m
   0 ——————————— 0.25 miles

1

GARWOL-DONG

Baekbeom-no

Wanhyo-ro

2

Samgakji Ⓢ

War Memorial
of Korea
◉1

Itaewon-ro

Yongho-ro

🔒 21

Yongsan
US Military
Base

Ⓢ Yongsan

3

Ⓢ Sinyongsan

3 ◉
Dragon
Hill Spa &
Resort

YEONGDEUNGPO-GU

4

**National
Museum
of Korea**
◉

Yongsan
Park

Ichon Ⓢ

Seobinggo-ro

5

Gangbyeon
Expwy

HAEBANGCHON

E   F   G   H

Hoenamu-ro

Hangangjin Ⓢ

16

Leeum Samsung
Museum of Art ⊙ 2   ⊗ 6

GYEONGRIDAN

Itaewon-ro 55-gil

HANNAM-DONG

🚻 15   🚻 12

20

22

Noksapyeong
Ⓢ

Noksapyeong-daero

Itaewon-ro
27ga-gil

17 18   ☆ 19

4 23

13 🚻   Ⓢ Itaewon

Noksapyeong Ⓢ

🔒 24   10

8 7 11   🚻 14

5

Itaewon-ro

Daesagwan-ro

⊗ 9

YONGSAN-GU

Usadan-ro

Usadan-ro 10-gil

Banpo-ro

Bogwang-ro

For reviews see	
⊙ Top Sights	p82
⊙ Sights	p88
⊗ Eating	p88
🚻 Drinking	p92
☆ Entertainment	p93
🔒 Shopping	p95

Han River
(Hangang)

Sights

War Memorial of Korea MUSEUM

1 Map p86, D2

This huge museum documents the history of the Korean War (1950–53) with heaps of black-and-white documentary footage (with English commentary) of the main battles and events. Along with photos, maps and artefacts, the films give a fascinating insight into what the war was like. There's plenty of military hardware outside – tanks, helicopters, missiles and planes, plus stirring war memorials. Time your visit to see the **Honour Guard Ceremony** (⏱2pm Fri early Apr–end Jun & mid-Oct–end Nov), an awesome display of military precision and weapon twirling by the armed forces. (전쟁기념관; www.warmemo.co.kr; 29 Itaewon-ro; admission free; ⏱9am-6pm Tue-Sun; ⑤Line 4 or 6 to Samgakji, Exit 12)

Leeum Samsung Museum of Art GALLERY

2 Map p86, H1

Korea's premier art gallery is divided into three main buildings, covering modern and traditional art. Contemporary-art lovers will want to focus on **Museum 2** featuring a mix of early- and midcentury paintings, sculptures and installations by esteemed Korean and international artists including Nam Jun Paik, Damien Hirst, Andy Warhol and Jeff Koons. For traditional Korean art, **Museum 1** is a must, with four floors of paintings, calligraphy, ceramics, celadon, metalwork and Buddhist art. The museum's third area is devoted to special exhibitions. (www.leeum.org; 60-16 Itaewon-ro 55-gil; adult/child ₩10,000/4000, temporary exhibition ₩7000/4000, day pass ₩13,000/6000; ⏱10.30am-6pm Tue-Sun; ⑤Line 6 to Hangangjin, Exit 1)

Dragon Hill Spa & Resort SAUNA

3 Map p86, A4

This foreigner-friendly *jjimjil-bang* – an upmarket sauna that's a noisy mix of gaudy Las Vegas bling and Asian chic – is one of Seoul's largest. In addition to the outdoor unisex pool, and all manner of indoor saunas and ginseng and cedar baths, there is a cinema, arcade games, beauty treatment rooms and multiple dining options. (드래곤힐스파; ☎010 -4223 0001; www.dragonhillspa.co.kr; 40-713, Hangangno 3(sam)-ga; day/night Mon-Fri ₩10,000/12,000, Sat & Sun all-day ₩12,000; ⏱24hr; ⑤Line 1 to Yongsan, Exit 1)

Eating

Vatos MEXICAN $

4 Map p86, F2

Tacos have long been popular as a snack of choice for GIs and expats in Itaewon but these guys make the shift from Tex-Mex to hipster LA food-truck-style tacos with a Korean twist. Expect soft corn tortillas filled with *galbi* (beef ribs), a side of 'kimchi *carnitas* fries' (fries with barbecued pork and kimchi) and cocktails such as its *'makgeolita'*. (☎02-797 8226; www.vatoskorea.com; 2nd

CHRISTIAN KOBER/GETTY IMAGES ©

Korean War Monument, War Memorial of Korea

fl, 1 Itaewon-ro 15-gil; 2 tacos from ₩6900; ⊘11.30am-11pm Sun-Thu, from noon Fri & Sat; 📶; **S** Line 6 to Itaewon, Exit 4)

PLANT
VEGAN $

5 Map p86, F2

Set up by the creator of the popular vegetarian blog **Aliens Day Out** (www. aliensdayout.com), this cosy vegan cafe specialises in dairy- and meat-free baked goods. The menu changes daily, but you can expect the likes of tempeh meatball subs, mock-chorizo pasta and awesome cakes such as salted-caramel pumpkin pie. (www.facebook.com/studioplant; 20 Itaewon-ro 16-gil; mains from ₩10,000; ⊘11am-8pm Tue-Sat; 📝; **S** Line 6 to Itaewon, Exit 4)

Passion 5
BAKERY, DESSERTS $

6 Map p86, H1

This homage to fine food is a good place to do a few laps of the gleaming arcade to check out a gourmet choice of goods from house-baked breads, sandwiches and soups (including a sourdough clam chowder), to hand-made chocolates and lavish cakes. There's also a Champagne bar and European-style deli items. (272 Itaewon-ro; sandwiches from ₩5000; ⊘7.30am-10pm; **S** Line 6 to Hangangjin, Exit 2)

Linus' BBQ
AMERICAN, BARBECUE $$

7 Map p86, F2

Specialising in authentic Southern-style American barbecue, Linus' does

Understand

Korean Food 101

Barbecue Most barbecue restaurants have a grill set into the tables on which to cook slices of *bulgogi* (beef), *galbi* (beef ribs), *samgyeopsal* (pork), *dak* (chicken), seafood or vegetables. The server often helps out with the cooking. These meals are usually only available in servings for two or more.

Rice Bibimbap is a tasty mixture of rice, vegetables and minced beef, often with a fried egg on top. Add *gochujang* (red-chilli paste) to taste and thoroughly mix it all together with a spoon before digging in. Similar to sushi rolls, are *gimbap* – rice rolled in dried seaweed with strips of carrot, radish, egg and ham in the centre.

Chicken *Samgyetang* is a small whole chicken stuffed with glutinous rice, red dates, garlic and ginseng root, and boiled in broth. Many informal *hof* (pubs) serve inexpensive barbecued or fried chicken to accompany beer.

Seafood Fish and other seafood is generally served broiled, grilled or in a soup, while *hoe* is raw fish like sashimi. *Twigin* (tempura) is also popular as a snack.

Vegetarian Although rice and vegetables make up a considerable part of their diet, few Koreans are fully vegetarian. Many seemingly vegetarian dishes have small amounts of meat, seafood or fish sauce added for flavour. The same is true of kimchi. Safer dishes for vegetarians to order include bibimbap (you'll need to request without meat, or egg), *beoseot-jeongol* (mushroom hotpot) or vegetable *pajeon* (pancake).

Soups & Stews *Tang* or *guk* (soups) are a highlight of Korean cuisine. They vary from spicy seafood and tofu soups to bland broths. *Jjigae* (stews) are usually served sizzling in a stone hotpot with plenty of spices.

Kimchi A cold side dish of the spicy national food is served at nearly every Korean meal, whether it's breakfast, lunch or dinner. It's generally made with pickled and fermented cabbage seasoned with garlic and red chilli.

Dumplings & Pancakes Dumplings can be filled with minced meat, seafood, vegetables and herbs. They are often freshly made, and fried, boiled or steamed. *Pajeon* are thick, savoury pancakes the size of pizzas, often filled with spring onions and seafood.

a range of Alabama- and Texan-style dishes which involves heaped plates of pulled pork or beef brisket, and excellent sandwiches. There's a *M*A*S*H* theme going (less tacky than it sounds) with its khaki canvas-covered terrace, combined with a 1950s Americana soundtrack. (www.facebook.com/linusbbq; 136-13 Itaewon-ro; mains from ₩15,000; ⊙11.30am-3.30pm & 5.30-10pm; ⓢLine 6 to Itaewon, Exit 4)

Suji's
AMERICAN $$

8 Map p86, F2

In a city where a decent Western breakfast is hard to find, this upstairs New York–style deli delivers. Grab a stool, a newspaper and go the well-priced egg-salad-muffin-coffee combo, or a full-scale greasy cook up. They also bake delicious cakes, and there are burgers and steaks on the menu. (www.sujis.net; 134 Itaewon-ro; breakfast from ₩3900, sandwiches from ₩15,000; ⊙8am-8.30pm; 🛜; ⓢLine 6 to Noksapyeong, Exit 2)

Bloc Party
BURGERS $$

9 Map p86, H3

On the hill among the artist community who've set up along Usadan-ro, this hole-in-the-wall bar-and-grill is run by a friendly New Yorker who knows how to do a mean cheeseburger. It has incredible views overlooking Hannam from its large gallery window. (www.facebook.com/blocpartyseoul; Usadan-ro 10-gil 51; mains from ₩12,000; ⊙noon-1am; ⓢLine 6 to Itaewon, Exit 3)

 Local Life

HBC Gogitjip

In the foreigner enclave of Haebang-chon, **HBC Gogitjip** (HBC고깃집; Map p86, E1; 46-5 Yongsandong 2-ga, Haebang-chon; meals ₩15,000-25,000; ⊙5pm-1am Mon-Fri, from 3pm Sat & Sun; 🛜; ⓢLine 6 to Noksapyeong, Exit 2) is popular among expats for its all-you-can-eat rib-eye Korean barbecue on Monday nights (₩15,000). But it's worth checking out any night of the week.

Bua
THAI $$

10 Map p86, G2

An ambience that succeeds in mixing classy with homely, Bua does authentic fragrant dishes from northern Thailand, as well as traditional and royal Thai cooked up by chefs from Chang Mai. Everything is made from scratch, including rotis and curry pastes using fresh ingredients. (2nd fl, 9 Bogwang-ro 59-gil; mains from ₩13,000; ⊙11.30am-3pm & 6-10pm Tue-Sat, 12.30-9.30pm Sun; ⓢLine 6 to Itaewon, Exit 4)

Lobster Bar
AMERICAN, SEAFOOD $$$

11 Map p86, F2

The hip and roomy upstairs Lobster Bar is packed with diners here to sink their teeth into soft, juicy lobster-filled rolls mixed with mayo, and melted butter with a side of fries. There's a good craft beer selection too. (www.lobsterbar.co.kr; 3rd fl, 140-1 Itaewon-ro; mains from ₩21,000; ⊙noon-10pm Mon-Sat, to 9pm Sun; ⓢLine 6 to Itaewon, Exit 4)

Drinking

Wolhyang
BAR

12 Map p86, H2

This upmarket *makgeolli* bar and restaurant has an interesting range of sweetened and unsweetened hand-crafted rice wines (₩9000 per litre) from around Korea. Go for its organic brown-rice *makgeolli*. Happy hour is from noon to 4pm. (월향; Taste of the Moon; http://tasteofthemoon.com; 13 Itaewon-ro 54-gil; ⏰noon-2am; ⑤ Line 6 to Hangangjin, Exit 3)

Venue/
CLUB

13 Map p86, F2

This dive-y basement club attracts a fun-loving, unpretentious crowd for quality DJs spinning hip hop and electronica. There's no cover charge, but there's a queue after midnight. (www. facebook.com/venuerok; 165-6 Itaewon-ro; ⏰10pm-6am; ⑤ Line 6 to Itaewon, Exit 1)

Four Seasons
BAR

14 Map p86, G2

Set up by a bunch of local beer geeks who brew their own ales, this base-ment bar has 10 craft beers on tap and a good stock of bottled varieties in the fridge. (사계; www.facebook.com/craftpub 4seasons; basement, 7 Bogwang-ro 59-gil; ⏰6pm-1am Mon-Thu, to 2am Fri, 2pm-2am Sat, to midnight Sun; ⑤ Line 6 to Itaewon, Exit 4)

Takeout Drawing
CAFE

15 Map p86, H2

This arty cafe is a cool place to hang out and enjoy graphic art, books, magazines and coffee with a twist (try the espresso with a spiky meringue topping), organic teas and other beverages. (www.takeoutdrawing.com; Itaewon-ro; 📶; ⑤ Line 6 to Hanganjjin, Exit 3)

Pet Sounds
BAR

16 Map p86, F1

Named after the young owner's love affair with the Beach Boys' *Pet Sounds* album, this popular upstairs rock bar provides a paper and pen to put in your requests to knowledgeable DJs. Has a good selection of drinks too. (www.facebook.com/petsoundsbar; 21 Hoenamu-ro; ⏰6pm-3am; ⑤ Line 6 to Noksapyeong, Exit 2)

Mowmow
BAR

17 Map p86, F2

There are usually a lot more brands of *makgeolli* (starting from ₩6500) to choose from than listed on the menu at this airy bar and eatery up the hill from the main Itaewon dining alley. Try one of the ₩9000 *makgeolli* cocktails. (모우모우; 54-3 Itaewon-ro 27ga-gil; ⏰3pm-3am; ⑤ Line 6 to Itaewon, Exit 1)

◯ Local Life
Itaewon 'Homo Hill'

Squished between 'Hooker Hill', 'Tranny Hill' and 'Halal Hill' (aka Little Arabia), 'Homo Hill' (Map p86, G2) is a 50m alley so-called because of its cluster of gay-friendly bars and clubs. All genders and sexual persuasions will feel welcome here.

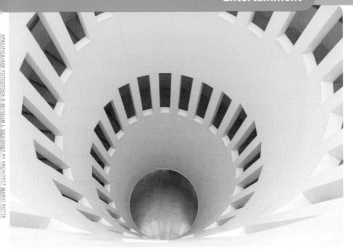

Interior, Leeum Samsung Museum of Art (p88)

B1   CLUB

18 📍 Map p86, G2

On the main drag, B1 is a good place to kick on to after the pub, and it's one of Itaewon's most well known clubs as evidenced by the long line to get in. (entrance Sat ₩10,000; ⊙8pm-4am Sun-Thu, 9am-5.30am Fri & Sat; ⑤ Line 6 to Itaewon, Exit 1)

Entertainment

All that Jazz   JAZZ

19 ☆ Map p86, G2

A fixture on the Seoul jazz scene since 1976, top local musicians regularly perform here; table reservations are recommended for the weekend. During the week live music starts at 8.30pm, with additional earlier 6.30pm shows on Fridays and weekends. There's also a late 11.30pm show on Friday and Saturday. (📞02-795 5701; www.allthatjazz.kr; 3rd fl, 12 Itaewon-ro 27ga-gil; admission ₩5000; ⊙6pm-1am Sun-Thu, to 2.30am Fri & Sat; ⑤ Line 6 to Itaewon, Exit 2)

Thunderhorse Tavern   LIVE MUSIC

20 ☆ Map p86, E2

Take the stairs down to this dingy basement venue for a regular roster of local and expat bands playing anything from indie and punk to metal. (www.thunderhorsetavern.com; Noksapyeong 220, Gyeongdiran; ⊙8.30pm-midnight; ⑤ Line 6 to Noksapyeong, Exit 2)

Understand

Confucianism

The state religion of the Joseon dynasty, Confucianism lives on as a kind of ethical bedrock for many Koreans, especially the elderly.

The Chinese philosopher Confucius (552–479 BC) devised a system of ethics that emphasised devotion to parents and family, loyalty to friends, justice, peace, education, reform and humanitarianism. As Confucianism trickled into Korea, it evolved into neo-Confucianism, which combined the sage's original ethical and political ideas with the quasi-religious practice of ancestor worship and the idea of the eldest male as spiritual head of the family.

Confucianism is a social philosophy, a prescription for achieving a harmonious society. Not everyone follows the rules, but Confucianism does continue to shape the Korean paradigm. Key principles and practices:

▶ Obedience and respect towards seniors – parents, teachers, the boss, older brothers and sisters – is crucial.

▶ Seniors get obedience, but they also have obligations. Older siblings help younger siblings with tuition fees, and the boss pays for lunch.

▶ Education defines a civilised person.

▶ Men and women have separate roles. A woman's role is service, obedience and management of household affairs. Men don't do housework or look after children.

▶ Status and dignity are critical. Every action reflects on the family, company and country.

▶ Everything on and beyond the earth is in a hierarchy. People never forget who is senior and who is junior to them.

▶ Families are more important than individuals. Everyone's purpose in life is to improve the family's reputation and wealth. No one should choose a career or marry someone against their parents' wishes – a bad choice could bring ruin to a family. Everyone must marry and have a son to continue the family line. For these reasons homosexuality is considered a grossly unnatural act.

▶ Loyalty is important. A loyal liar is a virtuous person.

▶ Be modest and don't be extravagant. Be frugal with praise.

Shopping

Yongsan Electronics Market
ELECTRONICS

21 🔒 Map p86, A2

If it plugs in, you can find it at this geeky universe of high-tech marvels. Computer prices are usually marked but prices on other goods are lacking, so do what the locals do – check out the prices online before arriving. It's also a good spot for well-priced (and barely used) secondhand phones. The area is being redeveloped, and is now spread across several buildings. (용산 전자랜드; 125 Cheongpa-ro; ⊘10am-7.30pm; ⑤Line 1 Yongsan, Exit 3)

Millimetre Milligram
STATIONERY, ACCESSORIES

22 🔒 Map p86, H2

Usually shortened to MMG, this is the spot to pick up quirky stationery and bags, including the Swiss brand Freitag. There's a cafe as well as a basement gallery/furniture store and, on the 3rd floor, the boutique art-book and magazine shop **Post Poetics** (www.postpoetics.org; 3rd fl, Itaewon-ro; ⊘1-8pm Mon-Sat). (www.mmmg.net; Itaewon-ro; ⊘11am-9pm; ⑤Line 6 to Itaewon, Exit 3)

Hamilton Shirts
FASHION

23 🔒 Map p86, F2

One of the larger and most reliable of the dedicated men's shirt makers that are clustered along Itaewon-ro, where you pick the material being fitted. A

🔍 Local Life
Stairway Flea Market

If the top of the hill near Seoul Central Mosque wasn't intriguing enough – with its extraordinary diversity mixing Seoul's Islamic community in among its GLBT community and red-light district – the enclave of artists who've relocated to Usadan-ro adds another layer of interest. Among the studios are galleries, pop-up shops and hole-in-the-wall bars and eateries. Visit on the last Saturday of each month for its **Stairway Flea Market** (Map p86, G3; Usadan-ro), with its street-party atmosphere.

Also, check out **HBC Art Village** (Map p86, E1; http://arthill100.com; ⑤Line 6 to Noksapyeong, Exit 2) in the adjoining suburb of Haebangchon, which has lively murals and art installations throughout its backstreets.

100% cotton shirt starts from ₩41,000. It also has a branch in Myeong-dong, and a store in Gangnam for women. (www.hs76.com; 153 Itaewon-ro; ⊘10am-7.30pm; ⑤Line 6 to Itaewon, Exit 1)

Eelskin Shop
ACCESSORIES

24 🔒 Map p86, F2

A good place to purchase ultrasoft eel-skin handbags, belts, wallets and purses. Eel-skin goods are an Itaewon speciality that make popular gifts. Wallets start at ₩15,000 and purses at ₩25,000. (Itaewon-ro; ⊘9.30am-8pm; ⑤Line 6 to Itaewon, Exit 4)

Top Sights
Demilitarized Zone (DMZ) & Joint Security Area (JSA)

Getting There

The only way to get here is by organised tour. Koridoor Tours and Panmunjom Travel Center are the two recommended tour operators. The DMZ is located 55km north of Seoul.

The 4km-wide, 240km-long buffer known as the Demilitarized Zone (DMZ) slashes across the peninsula, separating North and South Korea. Lined on both sides by tank traps, electrical fences, land-mines and armies in full battle readiness, it's one of the scariest and most surreal places on earth. It has become a major attraction, with several observatories allowing you to peek into North Korea. For history buffs and collectors of weird and unsettling experiences, a visit here is not to be missed.

Don't Miss

Joint Security Area (JSA)

The highlight of any trip to the DMZ is a visit to the JSA at Panmunjeom. It's here where the infamous Military Demarcation Line separates South and North Korea. The tension is palpable as soldiers from both sides stand metres apart eyeballing one another from their respective sides. You'll be taken inside the blue-painted UN meeting room – where the truce between North and South Korea was signed – the only place where you can safely walk into North Korea.

Dora Observatory

Peer through binoculars from here for a closer look at Kaesong city and Kaesong Industrial Complex in the DPRK (Democratic People's Republic of Korea; North Korea), where cheap North Korean labourers are employed by South Korean conglomerates.

Third Infiltration Tunnel

Since 1974 four tunnels have been found running under the DMZ, dug by the North Koreans so that their army could launch a surprise attack. Walking along 265m of this 73m-deep tunnel is not for the claustrophobic or the tall: creeping hunched over, you'll realise why they issue hard hats. The guide will point out how the North Koreans painted the rocks black so they might claim it was a coal mine!

Dorsan Train Station

Awaiting the next departure to Pyongyang (and onward Trans Eurasian intercontinental travel), Dorasan train station stands as a symbol of hope for the reunification of the two Koreas. The shiny new international customs built in 2002 remains unused. Trains to Seoul still run here four times daily.

Koridoor Tours

☎ 02-795 3028

www.koridoor.co.kr

tour ₩96,000

Ⓢ Line 1 to Namyeong, Exit 2

Panmunjom Travel Center

☎ 02-771 5593

http://panmunjomtour.com

6th fl, Lotte Hotel Main Bldg,

tours ₩77,000-120,000

Ⓢ Line 2 to Euljiro 1-ga, Exit 7 or 8

☑ Top Tips

▶ To visit the JSA, bring your passport.

▶ There are strict dress and behavioural codes; usually collared shirts for men, and no ripped jeans, revealing clothing or open-toed shoes.

▶ Only children over 10 years are permitted.

✗ Take a Break

If lunch isn't included in your tour, budget around ₩10,000 for lunch at the restaurant, or bring a packed lunch.

Explore

Gangnam & Apgujeong

Both flashy and ostentatious, Gangnam (meaning south of the river) is one of Seoul's ritziest districts. Despite its haughtiness and corporate environment, there's a lot to like about it, with some of Seoul's best shopping, restaurants, bars and clubs. Having received a makeover for the 1988 Olympics, it's a relatively new area with many high-rise apartments being developed in recent times.

The Sights in a Day

 Start the day with a coffee from one of Gangnam's artisan roasters such as **Steamers Coffee Factory** (p108). Wander among the peaceful royal tombs at **Seonjeongneung**, (p104) before checking out **COEX Mall** (p111) and its **aquarium** (p106). Across from here is the attractive **Bongeun-sa** (p103) Buddhist temple, a perfect antidote to Gangnam's extravagance.

For lunch dine on barbecued *galbi* (marinated beef) at **Samwon Garden** (p106), and browse boutiques along Apgujeong Rodeo St. Continue towards **Garosu-gil** (p101) for more shopping and have some fun at **K-Wave Experience** (p101). Alternatively, hit **Lotte World** (p103) amusement park and savour the views from atop **Lotte World Tower** (p105).

Arrive for your reservation at **Jungsik** (p107) for neo-Korean cuisine, then wander over to enjoy the Banpo Bridge Rainbow Fountain's nightly show (p103). Otherwise, take in *gugak* (traditional Korean music; p109) or a **ball game** (p110). You haven't really experienced Gangnam until you've partied at one of its megaclubs; **Club Octagon** (p107) is still the best.

For a local's day in Gangnam-gu, see p100.

 Local Life

Oppa Gangnam Style (p100)

 Best of Seoul

Getting There

S Subway Line 2 for Gangnam; Line 3 for Apgujeong; Bundang Line for Apgujeong Rodeo and Gangnam-gu

Local Life
Oppa Gangnam Style

It's as flashy as it gets in upscale Apgujeong, with all the excesses and trappings from Psy's 'Gangnam Style' on display. Checking out designer boutiques with eye-boggling price tags can be fun even if you lack the funds for purchases. This walk will lead you past all the big-name fashion stores, countless cosmetic surgeries and some K-Pop delights.

❶ K-Star Road
Gangnam's **'Halluwood Walk of Fame'** (Apgujeong Rodeo St; Ⓢ Line Bundang to Apgujeong Rodeo, Exit 7) pays homage to K-Pop stars in the form of cutesy bear sculptures dedicated to K-Wave singers and actors.

❷ Galleria
Department stores in Seoul don't get more luxurious than **Galleria** (✆02-344 9414; dept.galleria.co.kr; Apgujeong-ro,

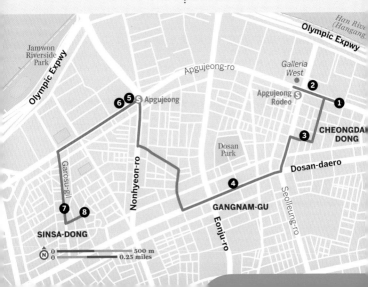

Gangnam-gu; ⊙10.30am-8pm; ⓢLine Bundang to Apgujeong Rodeo, Exit 7). If you want to play Audrey Hepburn staring wistfully into Tiffany's, don a Helen Kaminski hat, try on a Stella McCartney dress or slip into a pair of Jimmy Choos; the east wing of fashion icon Galleria is the place to be. The west wing is covered in glass discs that turn psychedelic at night.

3 Queens Park

This is the place for fashionistas to see and be seen. Run by the bakery behemoth Paris Croissant, **Queens Park** (✆02-542 4073; www.queens-park. co.kr; 22 Apgujeong-ro 60-gil, Gangnam-gu; mains ₩19,000-50,000; ⊙10am-midnight Mon-Fri, from 8am Sat & Sun; ⓢBundang Line to Apgujeong Rodeo, Exit 4) has a classy bakery section and dining area with a soaring ceiling and great design. For late risers it's perfect, as the brunch dishes, including an English breakfast, are available until 5.30pm.

4 313 Art Project

In the middle of Apgujeong's chic art hub, this slick **gallery** (www.313art project.com; 313 Dosan-daero, Gangnam-gu; ⓢLine 3 to Apgujeong, Exit 3) shows contemporary works by emerging and established artists, from both Seoul and abroad.

5 Hyundai Department Store

At **Hyundai** (www.ehyundai.com/lang/ en/index.do; 65 Apgujeong-ro, Gangnam-gu; ⊙10.30am-8pm; ⓢLine 3 to Apgujeong, Exit 6) you're greeted by uniformed doormen that exude old-fashioned elegance circa 1920s New York. It's mostly about high-end fashion and accessories. Head up to its food court for tasty *patbingsu* (red bean and fruit on milky shaved ice) at **Meal Top** (✆02-547 6800; Hyundai Department Store; desserts ₩7000; ⊙10.30am-10.30pm)

6 K-Wave Experience

Upstairs from the Gangnam Tourist Information Center, the **K-Wave Experience** (2nd fl, Gangnam Tourist Information Center, 161 Apgujeong-ro, Gangnam-gu; admission free; ⊙10am-7pm; ⓢLine 3 to Apgujeong, Exit 6) is *the* place to live out all your K-Pop fantasies. Here you'll get the full makeover to transform you into a K-Pop star, with a wardrobe of clothing, wigs and bling, as well as make-up, for that cheesy photo op. Also here is a bunch of CDs, DVDs and kitschy K-Wave souvenirs.

7 Garosu-Gil

One of Gangnam's most famous strips, this tree-lined street is worth a stroll for brand-name stores and cute fashion boutiques, plus art galleries, restaurants and cafes.

8 Lay Bricks

A popular hang-out with a passing array of characters – artists, models and hipsters – the industrial **Lay Bricks** (46 Nonhyeon-ro 153-gil, Gangnam-gu; ⊙11am-midnight Mon-Sat, from noon Sun; ⓢLine 3 to Sinsa, Exit 8) coffeehouse roasts its own beans and has a decent selection of craft beer too.

Han River
(Hangang)

Yongdong
Bridge

Olympic Expwy

Yeongdong-daero

Bongeunsa

Samseong S

Daechi S

Dogok S

500 m
0.25 miles

S Samseong

3
4
23

24

COEX
Aquarium

6

Samseong-ro

Hanti S

Cheongdam
Park

Cheongdam S

Samseong
Jungang

Seonjeongneung
Park

Yeoksam-ro

Seolleung S

Seolleung-ro

Dogok-ro

CHEONGDAM-
DONG

22

11
25

Seolleung-ro

Gangnam-gu
Office

Seonjeongneung

YEOKSAM-DONG

Teheran-ro

Yeoksam S

Apgujeong
Rodeo

7
20

Dosan
Park

8

Hakdong-ro

Eonju-ro

Bongeunsa-ro

Nonhyeon-ro

Dosan-daero

13

Apgujeong S

10

Nonhyeon-ro

SINSA-
DONG

Hak-dong

12

Nonhyeon-
DONG

GANGNAM-GU

Eonju S

Simnonhyeon

Gangnam S

Gangnam Tourist
Information Center

Apgujeong-ro

9

14

Garosu-gil

Hakdong
Park

Nonhyeon S

17

Gangnam-daero
(U-Street)

16

Sinsa S

15

SEOCHO-GU

Seocho-daero

Seoul National
University of
Education

Hannam S

Olympic Expwy

Hannam
Bridge

Jamwon

Gyeongbu Expwy

Banpo S

Sinbanpo-ro

Sapyeong-ro

Sapyeong S

Seochojungang-ro

Seocho S

Seocho-gu

19 21

5

Jamwon-ro

Umyeon-ro

BANPO-DONG

Express Bus
Terminal S

SEOCHO-GU

Seocho

Banpo
Bridge

Some Sevit
Jamwon
Riverside Park

Han River
(Hangang)

Banpo
Hangang
Park

Sinbanpo S

Sights

Bongeun-sa
BUDDHIST TEMPLE

1 Map p102, E2

Located in the heart of ritzy Gangnam, the shrines and halls of the Buddhist temple Bongeun-sa, with its tree-filled hillside location, stand in direct juxtaposition to its corporate high-rise surrounds. Founded in AD 794, the buildings have been rebuilt many times over the centuries. Entry to the temple is through **Jinyeomun** (Gate of Truth), protected by four king guardians. The main shrine, **Daewungjeon** has lattice doors and is decorated inside and out with Buddhist symbols and art that express Buddhist philosophy and ideals. (봉은사; ☑02-3218 4895; www.bongeunsa.org; 531 Bongeunsa-ro, Gangnam-gu; ⓢLine 2 to Samseong, Exit 6)

Some Sevit
ARCHITECTURE

2 Map p102, A2

At the south end of Banpo Bridge are these three artificial floating islands interconnected by walkways. Each features futuristic buildings in a complex that comprises restaurants, an exhibition hall and an outdoor stage. Definitely aim to visit at night when its buildings are lit up spectacularly by LED lights, as is the **Banpo Bridge Rainbow Fountain** (반포대교 달빛무지개분수; Banpo Bridge, Banpo-dong, Seocho-gu; admission free). (세빛섬; Sebitseom; www.somesevit.com; Hanggan

Top Tip

Temple Life
Make an effort to visit Bongeun-sa on a Thursday because from 2pm to 4pm monks and volunteers offer, in English, the **Templelife** (tour ₩20,000) program. This incorporates lotus-lantern making, *dado* (tea ceremony), a temple tour and Seon (Zen) meditation. There's also an opportunity to stay overnight in the two-day Templestay program (₩70,000), which includes activities and monastic meals; book three weeks in advance.

Riverside Park; admission free; ⓢLine 3, 7 or 9 to Express Bus Terminal, Exit 8-1)

Lotte World
AMUSEMENT PARK

3 Map p102, E3

This huge complex includes an amusement park, an ice-skating rink, a cinema multiplex, department store, folk museum, shopping mall, hotel, restaurants and more. Kids and adults alike will love the place, which is basically an indoor Korean version of Disneyland, complete with 'flying' balloons, 3D films, laser and music shows, screen rides, fantasy parades and thrill rides. The outdoor **Magic Island** is in the middle of Seokchon Lake, and that part may close in bad weather. (롯데월드; ☑02-1661 2000; www.lotteworld.com; 240 Olympic-ro, Songpa-Gu; adult/child/youth ₩31,000/25,000/28,000,

Understand
Royal Tombs of the Joseon Dynasty

The 40-odd royal tombs of the Joseon dynasty are World Heritage–listed and scattered across Seoul and Gyeonggi-do, with a couple also in the North Korean city of Kaesong. In these tombs, each similarly arranged on grassy mounds according to the rules of Confucianism and feng shui, are buried every Joseon ruler right up to the last, Emperor Sunjong (r 1907–10). Tomb entrances are marked by a simple red-painted wooden gate, stone pathway and hall for conducting rites in front of the humped burial mounds decorated with stone statuary – typically a pair of civil officers and generals, plus horses and protecting animals such as tigers and rams.

Seonjeongneung

The most central tomb in Seoul is Seonjeongneung, a **park** (Map p102, D4; ⊘6am to 8pm Tuesday to Sunday) that contains two main burial areas. The first is for King Seongjong (r 1469–94), who was a prolific author and father – he had 28 children by 12 wives and concubines. Go around the side and you can walk up to the tomb for a closer look. Nearby is the tomb of King Seongjong's second wife, Queen Jeonghyeon Wanghu.

A 10-minute walk further on through the thickly wooded park is the tomb of King Jeongjong (r 1506–44), the second son of King Seongjong and Queen Jeonghyeon. At this tomb you can see the full layout – the gateway and the double pathway to the pavilion where memorial rites were carried out – but you can't go near the tomb.

The park is open from 6am to 8pm from Tuesday to Sunday.

Donggureung

In Guri, around 20km northeast of central Seoul, is Donggureung. It's the largest and most attractive of the tomb complexes. Here lie seven kings and 10 queens, including the dynasty's founder King Taejo: in contrast to the other neatly clipped plots in this leafy park, his mound sprouts rushes from his hometown of Hamhung (now in North Korea) that – in accordance with the king's pre-death instructions – have never been cut. To reach the complex take subway line 2 to Gangbyeon to connect with bus 1, 1-1 or 1115-6, around a two-hour trip from central Seoul.

MAREMAGNUM/GETTY IMAGES ©

Bongeun-sa (p103)

passport incl most rides adult/child/youth ₩46,000/40,000/36,000; ⊘9.30am-10pm; ⑤Line 2 or 8 to Jamsil, Exit 3)

Lotte World Tower BUILDING

4 ◉ Map p102, E3

Due for completion in late 2016, Seoul's latest landmark is the 555m-high Lotte World Tower – the tallest skyscraper in Korea (and 6th highest in the world). Its sleek contemporary design is loosely inspired by traditonal Korean ceramics, and will feature the world's highest observation deck with a glass-floored skywalk, art gallery, cafe, six-star hotel and the mega Lotte World Mall (p110) complex. (www.lwt.co.kr/en/main.

do; 300 Olympic-ro, Songpa-gu; ⑤Line 2 or 8 to Jamsil, Exit 1)

Museum of Gugak MUSEUM

5 ◉ Map p102, B4

A part of the National Gugak Center (p109), this engaging museum covers *gugak* (traditional Korean music) with displays of Korean stringed instruments and unique drums among others that are rarely heard today. Some you're able to play, such as the Jeongak *gayaguem* (12-stringed zither dating from the Joseon dynasty). It's a five-minute walk from Seoul Arts Center. (✆02-580 3300; www.gugak.go.kr; National Gugak Center, 2364 Nambusunhwan-ro, Seocho-gu; admission free; ⊘9am-6pm

Tue-Sun; Line 3 to Nambu Bus Terminal, Exit 5)

COEX Aquarium

AQUARIUM

6 Map p102, E2

Seoul's largest aquarium exhibits thousands of fish and other sea creatures from around the world. You can see live coral, sharks, turtles, rays, electric eels, octopuses, evil-looking piranhas and pulsating jellyfish. Its only downside are the smallish enclosures for the seals and manatees. (02-6002 6200; www.coexaqua.com; COEX Mall, 513 Yeongdong-daero, Gangnam-gu; adult/child under 13yr/child 13-18yr ₩22,000/16,000/19,000; ⏱10am-8pm; ⑤Line 2 to Samseong, Exit 6)

Eating

Coreanos Kitchen

MEXICAN $

7 Map p102, D1

Originally a hipster food truck in Austin, USA, Coreanos (which is Spanish for Korean) brings its winning formula of kimchi tacos to Seoul. Tastes here are a fusion of authentic Mexican street food with Korean flavours, with its hand-pressed soft-corn tortilla tacos filled with anything from *galbi* (beef ribs) to kimchi pork belly. (www.coreanoskitchen.com; basement, 25 Seolleung-ro 157-gil, Gangnam-gu; tacos from ₩3300, burritos from ₩9000; ⏱noon-11pm; ⑤Bundang Line to Apgujeong Rodeo, Exit 5)

Nonhyeon Samgyetang

KOREAN $

8 Map p102, D2

The original branch of this popular restaurant is a good place to sample Korean specialities such as *samgyetang* (ginseng chicken soup) or steaming bowls of hearty *juk* (rice porridge) done with seafood or vegetarian servings. (720 Eonju-ro, Gangnam-gu; mains ₩8000-18,000; ⏱24hr; ⑤Line 7 to Hak-dong, Exit 10)

Gilbert's Burgers & Fries

BURGERS $$

9 Map p102, C1

From the moment those mouth-watering aromas of sizzling burgers hit you, there's no return from this underground diner which is a homage to American food. Its signature burger is the well-stacked Mr President, which comes with a 7oz (200g) beef patty. Wash it down with a good choice of American craft beers and sodas. (47 Dosan-daero 15-gil, Gangnam-gu; burgers from ₩10,000; ⏱11am-10pm Mon-Thu, 11.30am-11pm Fri-Sun; ⑤Line 3 to Sinsa, Exit 8)

Samwon Garden

KOREAN $$$

10 Map p102, C1

Serving top-class *galbi* for over 30 years, Samwon is a Korean idyll, surrounded by beautiful traditional gardens including several waterfalls. It's one of the best places in the city for this kind of barbecued-beef meal. There are also more inexpensive dishes such

GUITAR PHOTOGRAPHER/SHUTTERSTOCK ©

Banpo Bridge Rainbow Fountain (p103)

as *galbitang* (beef short-rib soup) for ₩13,000. (삼원가든; 📞02-548 3030; www.samwongarden.com; 835 Eonju-ro, Gangnam-gu; mains from ₩43,000; ⊙11.30am-10pm; Ⓢ Line 3 to Apgujeong, Exit 2)

Jungsik
NEO-KOREAN $$$

11 🍴 Map p102, D1

Voted number 10 in *Asia's 50 Best Restaurants* in 2015, neo-Korean cuisine hardly gets better than this. At the Apgujeong outpost of the New York restaurant named after creative chef-owner Yim Jungsik, you can expect inspired and superbly presented contemporary mixes of traditional and seasonal ingredients over multiple courses. Book at least one month in advance. (정식당; 📞02-517 4654; jungsik.kr; 11 Seolleung-ro, 158-gil, Gangnam-gu; 4-course lunch/dinner from ₩50,000/90,000; ⊙noon-3pm & 5.30-10.30pm; Ⓢ Bundang Line to Apgujeong Rodeo, Exit 4)

Drinking

Club Octagon
CLUB

12 🍸 Map p102, C2

Voted number six in the world's top clubs by *DJ Mag* in 2015, Octagon is one of Gangnam's best for serious clubbers. High-profile resident and guest DJs spin house and techno over its powerful Funktion 1 sound system to an appreciative crowd here to party till dawn. (www.cluboctagon.co.kr; 645 Nonhyeon-ro, Gangnam-gu; admission before 11pm & after 4am ₩10,000, after 11pm ₩30,000; ⏰10pm-6am Thu-Sat; §Line 7 to Hak-dong, Exit 4)

Moon Jar
BAR

13 🚻 Map p102, D1

Rustic charm meets Apgujeong chic at this convivial *makgeolli* (milky rice wine) bar and cafe spread over two floors. The menu has several different types of quality *makgeolli* served in kettles with the usual menu items such as *pajeon* (seafood pancakes). (달빛술담; 📞02-541 6118; 38 Apgujeong-ro 46-gil, Gangnam-gu; 750mL makgeolli from ₩7000; ⏰5.30pm-2am; 🛜; §Line 3 to Apgujeong, Exit 3)

Local Life
Neurin Maeul

The Gangnam branch of **Neurin Maeul** (느린마을 양조장; Map p102, C4; 📞02-587 7720; 7 Seocho-daero 73-gil, Seocho-gu; admission free; ⏰11am-11pm; §Line 2 to Gangnam, Exit 9), set up by Baesangmyeon Brewery, is a recommended place to sample traditional Korean alcohol. Its signature Neurin Maeul *makgeolli* (milky rice wine) is the standout – divided into the four 'seasons', which refers to the differing production stages; you can sample each before ordering. Jugs cost ₩8000 per litre (or ₩3000 take-away). You're likely to have to order food here.

Pongdang
MICROBREWERY

14 🚻 Map p102, C2

The original bar for this Korean microbrewery does a good selection of pale ales, Belgian and wheat beers, enjoyed at Pongdang's bar or tables surrounded by arcade machines. (www. pongdangsplash.com; 49 Apgujeong-ro 2-gil, Gangnam-gu; ⏰5pm-1am Sun-Thu, 4pm-2am Fri & Sat; §Line 3 to Sinsa, Exit 6)

Booth
BAR

15 🚻 Map p102, C4

A popular brew pub with its roots in Noksapyeong's Craft Beer Valley (p84), this Gangnam branch has several of its beers on tap, including its signature Bill's Pale Ale. It has a casual set-up of camping chairs, oil-drum tables and murals on the walls, and does pizza by the slice (₩4000). (www.theboothpub.com; 2nd fl, 11 Gangnam-daero 53-gil, Seocho-gu; beer from ₩5000; ⏰11.30am-1am; §Line 2 to Gangnam, Exit 5)

Steamers Coffee Factory
CAFE

16 🚻 Map p102, B1

Bringing third-wave coffee to Seoul, Steamers does Ethiopian and Colombian single-origin brews in its shabby-chic industrial brick cafe. (80 Dosan-daero 1-gil, Gangnam-gu; coffee ₩5000; ⏰8.30am-10pm Mon-Fri, from noon Sat; 🛜; §Line 3 to Sinsa, Exit 6)

PANYA K/SHUTTERSTOCK ©

Lotte World (p103)

Meakjugo
BAR

 17 Map p102, C3

Translating to 'Beer High School', this basement craft beer bar is done up in the theme of a 1980s Korean classroom. Grab a desk, and order from its top range of draft and bottled craft beers. Visit midweek for all-you-can-drink craft beer (₩12,900, two hours). (맥주고; 13 Gangnam-daero 96-gil, Gangnam-gu; ⊙5pm-2am; ⑤ Line 2 to Gangnam, Exit 11)

Ellui
CLUB

 18 Map p102, E1

If you're going to visit just one mega-club in Gangnam, Ellui is the one. It's a massive space with a dazzling light-and-sound system and multiple dance floors. (www.facebook.com/ellui.club; 551 Dosan-daero, Gangnam-gu; admission ₩30,000; ⊙10pm-8am Fri & Sat; ⑤ Line 7 to Cheongdam, Exit 13)

Entertainment

National Gugak Center
TRADITIONAL MUSIC

 19 Map p102, B4

Traditional Korean classical and folk music and dance are performed, preserved and taught at this centre, which is home to the Court Music Orchestra, the Folk Music Group, Dance Theater and Contemporary

Gugak Orchestra. The main theatre, Yeak-dang, puts on an ever-changing program by leading performers every Saturday, usually at 3pm. (☎02-580 3300; www.gugak.go.kr; 2364 Nambusunhwan-ro, Seocho-gu; tickets from ₩10,000; ⑤Line 3 to Nambu Bus Terminal, Exit 5)

Once in a Blue Moon   JAZZ

20 ⭐ Map p102, D1

An intimate and classy club with live jazz from two groups of performers every night, each playing two sets between 7.30pm and 12.30am. (원스인어 블루문; ☎02-549 5490; www.onceinablue moon.co.kr; 824 Seolleung-ro, Gangnam-gu; admission free; ◷6pm-1am; ⑤Bundang Line to Apgujeong Rodeo, Exit 4)

Seoul Arts Center   PERFORMING ARTS

21 ⭐ Map p102, B4

The national ballet and opera companies are based at this sprawling arts complex, which includes a circular opera house with a roof shaped like a

Korean nobleman's hat. It also houses a concert hall and a smaller recital hall in which the national choir, the Korea and Seoul symphony orchestras and drama companies stage shows. (예술의전당; SAC; ☎02-580 1300; www.sac.or.kr; 2406 Nambusunhwan-ro, Seocho-gu; tickets from ₩10,000; ⑤Line 3 to Nambu Bus Terminal, Exit 5)

Shopping

10 Corso Como Seoul   FASHION

22 🔒 Map p102, D1

Inspired by its shopping complex in Milan, this outpost of the fashion and lifestyle boutique is about as interesting as Gangnam retail can get. The blend of fashion, art and design includes several local designers. There's also a brilliant selection of international books and CDs to browse, and a chic cafe for an espresso or glass of wine. (www.10corsocomo.co.kr; 416 Apgujeong-ro, Gangnam-gu; ◷11am-8pm; ⑤Bundang Line to Apgujeong Rodeo, Exit 3)

Lotte World Mall   MALL

23 🔒 Map p102, E3

At the base of Korea's tallest building lies its largest shopping mall, comprising six floors of luxury and duty-free department stores, a mega cinema complex, concert hall and aquarium. There's also a department store at the nearby amusement park (p103). (www.lwt.co.kr/en/main.do; 300 Olympic-ro, Songpa-gu; ◷10.30am-10pm; ⑤Line 2 or 8 to Jamsil, Exit 1)

◯ Local Life
Jamsil Baseball Stadium

Even if you're not a baseball fan, it's worth coming along to **Jamsil Baseball Stadium** (admission ₩15,000-25,000; ⑤Lines 2 or 8 to Sports Complex, Exit 6) for its raucous, boozy atmosphere and for off-field entertainment such as K-Pop cheerleaders.

COEX Aquarium (p106)

COEX Mall

MALL

24 Map p102, E2

One of Seoul's premier malls, the shiny COEX is a vast maze of department stores loaded with shops selling fashion, lifestyle, accessories and electronics, as well as a multiplex cinema and aquarium (p106). It's also a launching point for the **CALT airport service** (☎02-551 0077; www. calt.co.kr; COEX Mall, 22 Teheran-ro 87-gil, Gangnam-gu; ⏰5.30am-6.30pm; Ⓢ Line 2 to Samseong, Exit 5), and has several hotels. (☎02-6002 5300; www.coexmall. com; 513 Yeongdongdae-ro, Gangnam-gu; ⏰10am-10pm; Ⓢ Line 2 to Samseong, COEX Exit)

Boon the Shop

CLOTHING

25 Map p102, D1

There are two close-by branches of this multibrand boutique that's a byword for chic, high-end fashion. The original, worth a look if only for its gorgeous sculpture of a giant string of pearls hanging in the midst of an atrium, is the women's store. Mainly exclusive niche designer brands from overseas; if you need to ask the price you can't afford to shop here. (☎02-2056 1228; www.boontheshop.com; 17 Apgujeong-ro 60-gil, Gangnam-gu; Ⓢ Bundang Line to Apgujeong Rodeo, Exit 4)

Top Sights
Olympic Park

Getting There

S Line 8 to Mongchontoseong, Exit 1

S Line 5 to Olympic Park, Exit 3

A focus of the 1988 Olympics, this large and pleasant park has an interesting variety of sights that make it worthy of a visit. As well as a place to stroll among greenery and lakes – past the Olympic sights – there's plenty here to see, from its modern art museum, and open-air sculptures to 3rd-century archaeological remains.

Don't Miss

Contemporary Art & Sculptures

Olympic Park's bunkerlike **SOMA** (소마미술관; Seoul Olympic Museum of Art; 02-425 1077; www.soma museum.org; adult/child ₩3000/1000; 10am-8pm Tue-Sun) features modern and contemporary art in six galleries. Most are special exhibitions covering local and big-name international artists such as Frida Kahlo. Check out the permanent video-art installations by Nam June Paik, and over 200 quirky sculptures scattered like buckshot around the park.

Museums

Seoul Baekje Museum (http://baekjemuseum.seoul.go.kr; Wiryeseong-daero; admission free; 9am-9pm Mon-Fri, to 6pm Sat & Sun) illuminates the history and culture of Hanseong (18 BC–AD 475), when this part of Seoul was the capital of the Baekje kingdom. Displays spread across three floors surround a full-scale model of workers constructing an earth rampart. There's also a walking-tour map that allows you to trace other Baekje sites in the area. Less interesting is the smaller **Mongchon Museum** (02-424 5138; admission free; 9am-6pm Tue-Sun), which exhibits precious golden relics of the Baekje kings and the usual ceramic pots.

Olympic Memorials

Standing at the main entrance is the colossal **World Peace Gate** (pictured), with its striking winged arches designed by Kim Jung-up for the 1988 Olympics as the centrepiece of the large Peace Plaza. The **Seoul Olympic Museum** (www.88olympic.or.kr; admission free; 10am-6pm Tue-Sun) relives the highlights of the 1988 Olympics with screens showing footage, together with a brief history of the games. Also here are many stadiums used during the Games, including the swimming pool, gymnastics hall and velodrome.

올림픽공원

www.olympicpark.co.kr

424 Olympic-ro, Songpa-gu

admission free

☑ Top Tips

▶ There's free **bicycle hire** (02-3431 3480; 8am-7pm Mar-Oct, 9am-5pm Nov-Feb; **S** Lines 2 or 8 to Jamsil, Exit 2) close to Jamsil subway station, a 200m walk southwards. Bring your passport.

✗ Take a Break

Within the main Olympic Park gate, **Seasons Table** (www.seasonstable.co.kr; Olympic Park; lunch weekday/weekend ₩13,900/22,900, dinner ₩22,900; 10am-10.30pm; **S** Line 5 to Olympic Park, Exit 3) is an earthy open-plan restaurant that buzzes with diners here for great-value all-you-can-eat Korean and fusion dishes. There's an excellent spread of traditional and seasonally based dishes of grilled meats, stews, and savoury pancakes, and good vegetarian options too.

Explore

Dongdaemun & Eastern Seoul

The sprawling, high-rise 24-hour shopping experience that is Dongdaemun is the largest of several market and mall precincts east of the city. You can shop for clothing, flea-market goods, antiques and herbal medicines further east. Dongdaemun Plaza offers dramatic contemporary architecture, while a stroll along a quieter section of the Cheong-gye-cheon is a pleasant way to reconvene with nature.

The Sights in a Day

Start off with the area's main sight, **Dongdaemun Design Plaza** (p116), exploring its inner workings and exhibitions, as well as its photogenic facade. Walk up a block or two to reach the **Seoul City Wall Museum** (p119), passing by the scenic **Heunginjimun** (p119) en route. Grab lunch from one of the food stalls within **Dongdaemun Market** (p122).

Take the subway east to **Seoul Yangnyeongsi Herb Medicine Market** (p125). Then walk south to Cheong-gye-cheon (Cheong-gye Stream) to visit **Cheonggyecheon Museum** (p119), which details the stream's interesting resurrection. Continue along the watercourse to **Seoul Folk Flea Market** (p124) for quality bric-a-brac. Jump back on the subway to **Gwangjang Market** (p124) for fried mungbean pancakes and bottle of *makgeolli* (milky rice wine).

Head back to Dongdaemun to see it lit up at night. K-Pop fans should check out the **Klive** (p123) hologram concert. Around the corner is Seoul's Central Asian community, 'Little Silk Road', where you can dine on lamb shashlik at **Samarkand** (p122) for dinner. Finish up at **Dongdaemun Market** (p124) to witness the shopping frenzy and snag a few bargains.

 Top Sights

Dongdaemun Design Plaza (p116)

 Best of Seoul

Eating

Gwangjang Market (p122)

Samarkand (p122)

Dongdaemun Market (p122)

Shopping

Dongdaemun Market (p124)

Seoul Folk Flea Market (p124)

Doota (p124)

Dapsimni Antiques Market (p125)

Entertainment

Klive (p123)

Getting There

S Subway Lines 2, 4 or 5 to Dongdaemun History & Culture Park; Lines 1 or 4 to Dongdaemun

Top Sights
Dongdaemun Design Plaza

Seoul's striking contemporary masterpiece, the Dongdaemun Design Plaza (DDP) is a showcase for Korean and international design. As well as its silver futuristic-looking building with streamlined free-flowing curves, it's a creative hub and cultural space home to galleries, event halls and design studios. Attached is the Dongdaemun History & Culture Park, with several museums that highlight past uses of this area, including a 16th-century military camp and a baseball stadium.

DDP; 동대문디자인플라자

👁 Map p118, C3

📞 02-2153 0408

www.ddp.or.kr

28 Eulji-ro, Jung-gu

🕙 10am-7pm Tue, Thu, Sat & Sun, to 9pm Wed & Fri

🚇 Line 2, 4 or 5 to Dongdaemun History & Culture Park, Exit 1

Don't Miss

Exterior

The DDP is architect Zaha Hadid's sleek concept dubbed the 'Metonymic Landscape'. The building, a curvaceous concrete structure with a silvery sci-fi facade, is fitted with LED lights that pulsate meditatively at night. Its undulating layout leads to public spaces, convention centres and an underground plaza as well as lawns that rise up on to its roof.

Interior & Exhibitions

The interior of this cultural complex is equally impressive. Its amorphous structure is filled with floors of galleries, exhibition spaces, design shops and studios interconnected by long flowing pathways and sculpted staircases. Ticket prices for exhibitions range from free to ₩10,000.

Dongdaemun History Museum

During the site's excavation, major archaeological remains from the Joseon dynasty were uncovered, including original sections of the Seoul City Wall. The remains have been incorporated into the park and include the arched floodgate Yigansumun. The **Dongdaemun History Museum** (Dongdaemun Design Plaza; admission free; ⏱10am-7pm) imaginatively displays the pick of the 2575 artefacts from the site and provides the historical background to the ancient foundations preserved outside. Look for the patterned section of pavement made from clay tiles.

Dongdaemun Stadium Memorial

The Dongdaemun Stadium Memorial re-lives key moments from the stadium's history. Built by the Japanese in 1925, it was used for soccer and baseball matches until it was demolished in 2007. Several of the stadium floodlights remain standing.

☑ Top Tips

▶ Tours of the complex can be arranged by calling ahead.

✖ Take a Break

Just across from the DDP is the 'Dongdaemin Silk Road', home to Seoul's small Central Asian community, with plenty of great restaurants including Samarkand (p122).

Head to Dongdaemun Market (p122) for street food or small restaurants selling anything from skewered meats and smoked mackerel to barbecue dishes.

E

◉ 5
14 ◉
◉ 3
4 ◉ Sangwangsimni
◉ 12

◉ 10 ◉ Ⓢ
Sinseol-dong

Jungang
Market

Seoul Art
Space
Sindang

DONGDAEMUN-GU

Ⓢ Dongmyo

Ⓢ Dongmyo
Dasan-ro
Ⓢ Sindang

Majang-ro

D

Cheong-gye-cheon

Fashion Wholesale
& Retail Area

Ⓢ Cheonggu
Dasan-ro

C

◉ 1
Ⓢ Heunginjimun
Seoul City
Wall Museum
Ⓢ Dongdaemun

✕ 8

Dongdaemun
History &
Culture Park

**Dongdaemun
Design Plaza** ◉

13 ◉

GWANGHUI-DONG

Ⓢ

Jangchungdan-ro

Dongdaemun
History &
Culture Park Ⓢ
🍴 11
✕ 7

B

Jongno 5-ga Ⓢ

Daehak-ro
Dongho-ro

Eulji-ro

Jungbu
Market

Mareunnae-ro

Dongguk
University Ⓢ
Toegye-ro

Dongguk
Janchungdan

500 m
0.25 miles

◉ 6 ✕

✕ 9

Changgyeonggung-ro

Dongguk

A

N

1

2

3

4

Sights

Seoul City Wall Museum   MUSEUM

1 ⊙ Map p118, C2

On the Naksan Park hill overlooking Heunginjimun (Dongdaemun), near a stretch of the Seoul City Wall, this modern museum offers an engaging history of the 18.6km-long wall that surrounds the city. There are plenty of high-tech interactive displays, combined with artefacts from the original wall and a model of Sungnyemun built from Lego. (한양도성박물관; ☑02-724 0243; seoulcitywall.seoul.go.kr; 283 Yulgok-ro, Jongno-gu; admission free; ◷9am-7pm Tue-Sun; ⑤Line 1 or 4 to Dongdaemun, Exit 1)

Heunginjimun   GATE

2 ⊙ Map p118, C2

The Great East Gate to Seoul's City Wall has been rebuilt several times in its 700-year history and, after recent renovations, today it's looking majestic. Stranded in a traffic island, it's not possible to enter inside the gate; but there's plenty of good photo ops from Naksan Park. (Dongdaemun; ⑤Line 1 or 4 to Dongdaemun, Exit 6)

Cheonggyecheon Museum   MUSEUM

3 ⊙ Map p118, E2

To fully comprehend what a mammoth and expensive effort it was to resurrect Seoul's long-covered-over Cheong-gye-cheon, pay a visit to this well-designed museum about the stream. It's a good starting point for a walk along the riverside park. Across from here is the **Cardboard House Museum** (Cheong-gyecheon-ro, Seongdong-gu; admission free; ◷10am-8pm Tue-Sun; ⑤Line 2 to Yongdu, Exit 5), a wooden shack that was typical of the slum houses that used to line the river back in the 1950s. It displays paraphernalia of Seoul dating from this period of time. (청계천박물관; ☑02-2286 3434; www.cgcm.go.kr; 530 Cheonggyecheon-ro, Seongdong-gu; admission free; ◷9am-7pm Tue-Sun; ⑤Line 2 to Yongdu, Exit 5)

Children's Grand Park   PARK

4 ⊙ Map p118, E3

Let your little ones run wild in this enormous playground, which includes amusement rides, a zoo, botanical garden, wetland eco area and a giant musical fountain. (서울 어린이대공원;

Local Life
Seoul Art Space Sindang

In the underground arcade that runs beneath the Jungang Market a collection of design and art studios called **Seoul Art Space Sindang** (Map p118, D2; http://english.sfac.or.kr; Sindang Underground Shopping Center, 87 Majang-ro, Jung-gu; admission free; ◷10am-6pm; ⑤Line 2 to Sindang, Exit 1 or 2) has popped up. As part of a citywide project to foster up-and-coming artists, sections of the arcade have been turned into a gallery of the artists' work, which shares space with raw seafood restaurants.

Understand

Traditional Korean Arts

Visual Arts

Chinese influence is paramount in traditional Korean painting. The basic tools (brush and water-based ink) are those of calligraphy, which influenced painting in both technique and theory. The brush line, which varies in thickness and tone, is the most important feature. Traditional landscape painting is meant to surround the viewer, and there is no fixed viewpoint as in traditional Western painting. Court ceremonies, portraits, flowers, birds and traditional symbols of longevity were popular subjects.

Music

Gugak (Korean traditional music) is played on stringed instruments, most notably the *gayageum* (12-stringed zither) and *haegum* (two-stringed fiddle) as well as on chimes, gongs, cymbals, drums, horns and flutes. *Jeongak* (court music) is slow and stately, while folk music such as *samullori* is fast and lively. Similar to Western opera is *changgeuk*, which can involve a large cast of characters. An unusual type of opera is *pansori*. It features a solo storyteller (usually female) singing to the beat of a drum, while emphasising dramatic moments with a flick of her fan. The singing is strong and sorrowful.

Literature

During the Joseon dynasty, literature meant *sijo*, short nature poems that were handwritten (using a brush and ink) in Chinese characters, even after the invention of *hangeul* (the Korean phonetic alphabet) in the 15th century. In the 20th century, however, there was a sharp turn away from Chinese (and Japanese) influence of any kind. Western ideas and ideals took hold, and existentialism and other international literary trends found footing, but through a unique and pervasive Korean lens.

Theatre & Dance

Korean folk dances include dynamic *seungmu* (drum dances), the satirical and energetic *talchum* (mask dances) and solo *salpuri* (shamanist dances). Most popular are *samullori* dance troupes, who perform in brightly coloured traditional clothing, twirling a long tassel from a cap on their heads at the same time as they dance and beat a drum or gong.

Seoul Yangnyeongsi Herb Medicine Market (p125)

☎02-450 9311; www.childrenpark.or.kr; 216 Neungdong-ro, Gwangjin-gu; rides ₩4000; ⏰5am-10pm, park 9am-5pm, zoo 10am-6pm; Ⓢ Line 5 or 7 to Children's Grand Park, Exit 1)

Seoul Yangnyeongsi Herb Medicine Museum
MUSEUM

5 ◎ Map p118, E1

Learn about the history and practice of traditional Korean medicine at this imaginative museum. The displays have plenty of English, and the kind ladies here will give you herbal tea and allow you to work out which *sasang* constitution you have. To get here take a left at the subway and look for the building with a big Korean flag on it – it's located a bit back from this. (서울약령시 한의약박물관; ☎02-3293 4900; http://museum.

ddm.go.kr; B2 Donguibogam Tower, 128 Wangsan-ro, Dongdaemun-gu; admission free; ⏰10am-6pm Tue-Sun; Ⓢ Line 1 to Jegi-dong, Exit 3)

Local Life
Seoul Forest

A hunting ground in Joseon times, **Seoul Forest** (서울숲; http://parks.seoul. go.kr; 685 Seongsu1-ga 1-dong, Seongdong-gu; ⏰rental stall 9am-10pm; Ⓢ Bundang Line 2 to Seoul Forest, Exit 2) makes for a pleasant way to enjoy nature. It's big, so to see it all it's best to hire a bicycle (₩3000 per 1½ hours) or a pair of rollerblades (₩4000 per hour) from the rental stall by Gate 2 across from the subway. Among the trees and lakes are deer enclosures, eco areas and a butterfly house.

Eating

Gwangjang Market
KOREAN $

 6 Map p118, A2

Best known as Seoul's largest food alley (or *meokjagolmok*), Gwangjang Market (p124) is home to some 200 stalls set up among kimchi and fresh seafood vendors. Its speciality is the golden fried *nokdu bindaetteok* (mungbean pancake; ₩5000) – paired beautifully with *makgeolli*. Otherwise go a more healthy option of bibimbap or *boribap* (mixed rice and barley topped with a selection of vegies). (광장시장; Kwangjang; www.kwangjangmarket.co.kr; 88 Changgyeonggung-ro, Jongno-gu; dishes ₩4000-10,000; ⊘8.30am-10pm; S Line 1 to Jongno 5-ga, Exit 8, or Line 2 or 5 to Euljiro 4-ga, Exit 4)

Dongdaemun Market
MARKET $

 8 Map p118, B2

Within the Dongdaemun Shopping Complex of the main market (p124), here there's an excellent choice of street food from vendors to small

Top Tip

Dongdaemun at Night

It's worth returning to Dongdaemun's main shopping district in the evening, when it takes on a electrifying atmosphere as shoppers descend en masse and buildings blaze with dazzling neon.

restaurants, including several that specialise in charcoal barbecued *samchi* (Spanish mackeral). (동대문시장; dishes from ₩6000; ⊘10am-10pm; S Line 1 or 4 Dongdaemun, Exit 8)

Samarkand
CENTRAL ASIAN $$

7 Map p118, B3

This family-run Uzbekistan restaurant is a part of Dongdaemun's 'Little Silk Road', an intriguing district that's home to a community of Russian-speaking traders from the 'Stans, Mongolia and Russia. It has delicious halal home-cooking, including lamb shashlik that goes beautifully with fresh *lepeshka* bread and Russian beer. The area is worth a look around; signage is in Cyrillic. (사마르칸트; 159-10 Mareunnae-ro, Jung-gu; mains from ₩8000; ⊘10am-11pm; S Line 2, 4 or 5 to Dongdaemun, Exit 12)

Woo Rae Oak
NOODLES, BARBECUE $$

9 Map p118, A2

Tucked away in the sewing-machine parts section of Dongdaemun's sprawling market streets is this elegant old-timer specialising in *bulgogi* and *galbi* (barbecued beef; from ₩29,000, could feed two). But its delicious *naengmyeon* (buckwheat cold noodles) make the best lunch paired with delicious kimchi. (우래옥; ☎02-2265 0151; 62-29 Changgyeonggung-ro, Jung-gu; mains ₩11,000-43,000; ⊘11.30am-10pm; S Line 2 or 4 to Euljiro 4-ga, Exit 4)

Understand
K-Pop

Dating back to the 1990s boy bands in Seoul, Korean pop (K-Pop) has been at the forefront of the Korean Wave (aka Hallyu) well before Psy started busting out his crazy moves. The popularity of K-Pop has reached fanatical levels among devotees in Korea, China and Japan, and this has extended into a world-wide phenomenon with fans from the Middle East to Latin America.

But of course it was in 2012, with Psy's smash hit 'Gangnam Style', when things really exploded. Topping the charts in nearly 30 countries, the song single-handedly thrust K-Pop into the spotlight of Western countries and still remains the world's most viewed YouTube clip, as of 2015.

Fans of K-Pop will have ample opportunity to enjoy tunes – both recorded and live – by their favourite singers and bands in Seoul. Other than Psy, among solo singers, few have attained the level of commercial success of BoA and her male counterpart Rain. Among the current-day K-Pop acts, popular ones include boy bands EXO, Bigbang, SHINee, the 13-member group Super Junior, and girl bands Wonder Girls and Girls' Generation.

Drinking

Hidden Track   BREWERY

 10 🍺 Map p118, E1

Set up by the BBB Brewing Company, this basement microbrewery pub serves five of its own beers on tap including the signature IPA and a few German-style beers. The brewing vats sit behind the bar. It's a 10-minute walk south from Anam subway, located just off the roundabout. (숨겨진음악; www.facebook.com/hiddentrack; 6 Yangnyeongsi-ro, Dongdaemun-gu; beers from ₩5000; ⏱6pm-1am Mon-Sat; ⑤Line 6 to Anam, Exit 3)

Entertainment

Klive   LIVE PERFORMANCE

11 ⭐ Map p118, B3

One for the K-Pop fans out there, with nightly concerts using state-of-the-art hologram technology with scarily real effects. It's all in Korean, but there are English subtitles. (☎02-2265 0810; www.klive.co.kr; 9th fl, Lotte Fitin Bldg, 264 Eulji-ro, Jung-gu; adult/child ₩33,000/16,000; ⏱shows 2pm, 4pm, 6pm & 8pm Tue-Sun; ⑤Line 2, 4 or 5 to Dongdaemun History & Culture Park, Exit 11)

Shopping

Dongdaemun Market
MARKET

Take Seoul's commercial pulse at this colossal retail and wholesale market (see 8 ✕ Map p118, B2). It sprawls across a wide area on both sides of the Cheong-gye-cheon. On one side is the multilevel **Pyoung Hwa Clothing Market** (평화시장; Dongdaemun Market; ⏱7pm-10pm) crammed with stalls selling wholesale clothing and accessories. On the other side of the stream is **Dongdaemun Shopping Complex** (Dongdaemun Market; ⏱9am-6pm Mon-Sat), with a more eclectic range of goods, plus atmospheric food alleys (p122). (동대문시장; Dongdaemun; ⏱7-10pm Mon-Sat; Ⓢ Line 1 or 4 to Dongdaemun, Exit 8)

Local Life
Jungang Market

One of Seoul's oldest markets, **Jungang** (서울중앙시장; Map p118, D2; 87 Majang-ro, Jung-gu; dishes from ₩6000; ⏱noon-4pm Mon-Sat; Ⓢ Line 2 to Sindang, Exit 1 or 2) is very much a local affair, with vendors selling street food, kimchi and fresh produce. Seafood is a speciality here, from *samchi* (grilled Spanish mackerel) and *haemul pajeon* (seafood pancake) to *hoe* (raw fish dish) restaurants in the underground arcade section, where you can also check out Seoul Art Space Sindang (p119).

Seoul Folk Flea Market
MARKET

12 🔒 Map p118, E1

Spilling out of a two-storey building into the surrounding area, here you'll find a fascinating collection of artworks, collectables and general bric-a-brac from wooden masks and ink drawings to Beatles LPs and valve radios. (서울풍물시장; 19-3 Cheonho-dae-ro 4-gil, Dongdaemun-gu; ⏱10am-7pm, closed 2nd & 4th Tue of month; Ⓢ Line 1 or 2 to Sinseol-dong, Exit 6 or 10)

Doota
DEPARTMENT STORE

13 🔒 Map p118, B2

Cut through Dongdaemun's commercial frenzy by heading to its leading fashion mall full to the brim with domestic brands. Ten floors above and below ground are dedicated to clothing, accessories, beauty items and souvenirs. When you start flagging, there are plenty of cafes and a good food court on the 7th floor. (☎02-3398 3114; www.doota.com; 275 Jangchungdan-ro, Jung-gu; ⏱10.30am-midnight Sun-Thu, to 5am Fri & Sat; Ⓢ Line 2, 4 or 5 to Dongdaemun History & Culture Park)

Gwangjang Market
CLOTHING

As well as the food (p122) and fabrics sold here (see 6 ✕ Map p118, A2), head upstairs for vintage secondhand clothing stalls. There's the usual flannel shirts, vintage dresses, army jackets, sunglasses and Doc Martens, mixed in with some local fashion. Access is by

Food stalls at Gwangjang Market (p122)

the stairs to the upper floor outside exit 2. (광장시장; 2nd & 3rd fl, West Gate 2, 88 Changgyeonggung-ro, Jongno-gu; ⏰10am-7pm Mon-Sat, from 11am Sun; Ⓢ Line 1 to Jongno 5-ga, Exit 8 or Line 2 or 5 to Euljiro 4-ga, Exit 4)

Seoul Yangnyeongsi Herb Medicine Market   MARKET

Also known as Gyeongdong Market, Korea's biggest Asian medicine market (see 5 ⊙ Map p118, E1) runs back several blocks from the traditional gate on the main road and includes thousands of clinics, retailers, wholesalers and medicine makers. If you're looking for a leaf, herb, bark, root, flower or mushroom to ease your ailment, it's bound to be here.

(www.seoulya.com; Jegi-dong; ⏰9am-7pm; Ⓢ Line 1 to Jegi-dong, Exit 2)

Dapsimni Antiques Market   ANTIQUES

14 🔒 Map p118, E1

For serious collectors, this sprawling collection of antique shops is spread over three separate precincts. Here you can browse through old dusty treasures – from *yangban* (aristocrat) pipes and horsehair hats to wooden shoes, fish-shaped locks and embroidered status insignia. Items are anywhere between 100 and 600 years old. (⏰10am-6pm Mon-Sat; Ⓢ Line 5 to Dapsimni, Exit 2)

The Best of
Seoul

Seoul's Best Walks

Seoul's Best...

Dongdaemun Design Plaza (p116)
MAREMAGNUM/GETTY IMAGES ©

Best Walks
Namsan to City Hall

🏃 The Walk

Combining mountain trails with plenty of Joseon-era history, traditional and modern culture, and delicious food, this walk showcases downtown Seoul. Take the cable car up past the Seoul City Wall to Namsan to enjoy sweeping views and fresh air. Admire the city from atop N Seoul Tower, before descending down the mountain to Namdaemun Market for a lively atmosphere and delicious food. Moving along you'll see fantastic contemporary artwork before exploring the 16th-century palace, and a fascinating mix of colonial and contemporary architecture.

Start Namsan Upper Cable-Car station; **S** Line 4 to Myeongdong, Exit 3

Finish City Hall; **S** Line 1 or 2 to City Hall, Exit 5

Length 2.5km; three hours

🍴 Take a Break

Head to the food alley near Gate 5 at Namdaemun Market for the cluster of indoor stalls cooking up fresh, cheap and tasty bibimbap.

SANTI RODRIGUEZ/GETTY IMAGES ©

Seoul City Hall (p54)

❶ Namsan & N Seoul Tower

Take the **cable car** (p47), or follow the path up past the Seoul City Wall, to the top of Namsan – enjoying the fresh air, forested hills and shrines along the way. At the top of Namsan, zip up the 236m **N Seoul Tower** (p46) to enjoy incredible skyline views.

❷ Sungnyemun

The park continues over a road tunnel down past sections of the wall, leading to the recently renovated **Sungnyemun** (p49). The majestic Joseon-era gate was first erected in the 14th century, and stands out grandly among its 21st-century surrounds.

❸ Namdaemun Market

Cross the road to the sprawling **Namdaemun Market** (p48), the largest in Korea. Join the sea of shoppers to browse stalls selling clothing, accessories and souvenirs. Head down one of the food alleys for a delicious Korean meal.

❹ PLATEAU

A short stroll up from the market is the classy **PLATEAU** (p56) gallery. Its monthly shows exhibit works by local contemporary artists and are always worth a look. The magnificent lobby features two epic pieces by master sculptor Auguste Rodin.

❺ Seoul Museum of Art

Further along you'll arrive at the former foreign legation quarter of Seoul. Established during the late 1900s, there are many examples of colonial architecture to be seen, including the 1928 former courthouse, which now houses the **Seoul Museum of Art** (p55) – one of the city's finest modern-art galleries.

❻ Deoksugung

A few twists and turns ahead is one of Seoul's most famous **palaces** (p50). Used off and on as the king's residence from the 16th century, it's the last palace used during the Joseon dynasty. It's notable for its mix of colonial and traditional architecture.

Time your arrival for the changing-of-the-guard ceremony, held three times a day.

❼ City Hall & Seoul Plaza

Cross the road to reach another city landmark: **Seoul City Hall** (p54), with its striking glass-wave facade. Head down to the basement for multimedia art exhibitions. It's adjoined by the Seoul Metropolitan Library, a renaissance-style building with an iconic clock, which looks over the grassy **Seoul Plaza** (p54).

Best Walks
Insa-dong & Palaces

🏃 The Walk

Take a trip back through time to the Joseon dynasty on this walk that leads you to some of Seoul's best palaces, Confucian shrines and Buddhist temples. Along the way you'll drop by traditional teahouses, galleries, bars, and shops selling quality handicrafts, among the maze-like backstreets full of *hanok* (traditional houses).

Start Jogye-sa; **S** Line 3 to Anguk, Exit 6

Finish Changdeokgung; **S** Line 3 to Anguk, Exit 3

Length 1.5km; three hours

🍴 Take a Break

For delicious steaming bowls of Pyongyang-style dumplings, head to Koong (p38). Alternatively, treat yourself to a classy meal at Min's Club (p39).

Architectural detail, Jogye-sa (p28)

① Jogye-sa

Kick off with a visit to the Zen Buddhist temple at **Jogye-sa** (p28). Built in 1938, its main temple building, Daeungjeon, features colourful murals from scenes of Buddha's life as well as three giant Buddha statues. Within the grounds are several halls and pavilions, and a Buddhist museum with changing exhibits.

② KCDF Gallery

For wonderful souvenirs, pop into **KCDF Gallery** (p41) for quality pottery, jewellery and other handmade crafts. Head to the basement of the KCDF building for a prearranged tour at **Sool Gallery**, which gives a rundown on traditional Korean alcohols and includes samples of *makgeolli* (milky rice wine), *soju* (vodka) and *yakju* (refined rice wine).

③ Insa-dong Maru

A modern complex of artisan shops, **Insa-dong Maru** (p41) sells anything from handmade shoes and handicrafts to designer watches.

④ Dawon

In the warren of alleyways you'll hopefully

stumble upon **Dawon** (p40), a lovely *hanok* teahouse with a tree-filled courtyard and a wonderful assortment of traditional teas.

⑤ Sik Mool

Make your way out of the touristy area to **Sik Mool** (p40). Comprising four adjoining *hanok,* this bar mixes contemporary art and Soviet propaganda posters with pizza, a good selection of cocktails, wine and coffee.

⑥ Unhyeongung

The former childhood residence of King Go-jong (before he ascended the throne aged 12), the palace of **Unhyeongung** (p36) is a nice place for a wander. Take in the furnished living quarters and exhibition hall, and hopefully a music performance too. If you're in the mood, you can also try on *hanbok* (traditional clothing).

⑦ Jongmyo

Continue east to the World Heritage–listed stop at **Jongmyo** (p34), a Confucian shrine that's another beautiful display of traditional Korean architecture. It contains 49 royal spirit tablets in 19 small rooms, which are believed to contain the spirits of Joseon kings and queens.

⑧ Changdeokgung

Built in 1405 **Changdeokgung** (p26) served as the palace for many Joseon-dynasty kings. It's Seoul's most beautiful and well-preserved palace, set among huge grounds full of gardens, halls, pavilions and ponds. Note that the only way to visit is by guided tour, so time your run to get here for the 2.30pm English tour.

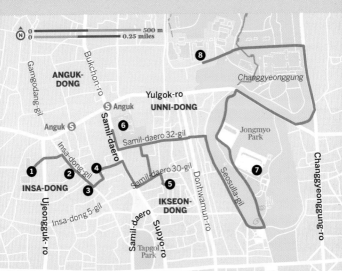

Best Walks
Dongdaemun

🏃 The Walk

Where modern and contemporary Seoul collide head on, this lively shopping district features Joseon-dynasty landmarks among cutting-edge contemporary architecture. From history buffs and modern-art lovers to shopaholics, there's something for everyone on this stroll.

Start Jungdang Market; **S** Line 2 to Sindang, Exit 1 or 2

Finish Dongdaemun Design Plaza; **S** Line 2, 4 or 5 to Dongdaemun History & Culture Park, Exit 1

Length 1km; 2½ hours

🍴 Take a Break

For something different, venture into Seoul's 'Little Silk Road' Central Asian precinct, where Cyrillic script is more common than *hangeul* (Korean phonetic alphabet). The Ubzek restaurant Samarkand (p122) does delicious lamb shashlik and home-baked breads.

Dongdaemun Market (p124)

❶ Jungang Market & Seoul Art Space

One of Seoul's oldest markets, **Jungang** (p124) is a traditional arcade, with stalls of food, kimchi and fresh produce. Take the stairs down to **Seoul Art Space Sindang** (p119), where local artists and designers have set up their studios among the raw-fish restaurants.

❷ Cheong-gye-cheon

A raised highway was demolished and the ground dug up to 'daylight' this long-buried **stream** (p34). It transformed Seoul's centre, creating a riverside park and walking course that's a calm respite from the surrounding commercial hubbub. Public art is dotted along the banks.

❸ Heunginjimun

A facelift to **Heunginjimun** (p119; aka Dongdaemun) has left the old 14th-century east gate to the city looking grander than it has done in decades. It's permanently locked

SEONGJOON CHO/GETTY IMAGES ©

from the outside, but you'll get some great photos.

❹ Seoul City Wall Museum

Appropriately backing on to a section of Seoul's 14th-century wall, the snazzy **Seoul City Wall Museum** (p119) details the wall's history through multimedia displays. As well as relics from the original wall, there's also a model of Sungnyemun made from Lego.

❺ Dongdaemun Market

Bisected by Cheong-gye-cheon, the **Dongdaemun Market** (p124) is divided into two sections. Most famous is the multi-level wholesale **Pyoung Hwa Clothing Market**, good for bargain items. On the other side of the stream, **Dongdaemun Shopping Complex** is good for street-market food. Venture further south towards the DDP for better quality fashion malls.

❻ Dongdaemun Design Plaza (DDP)

The final stop of the walk climaxes with the **DDP** (p116). Designed by Iraqi-British architect Zaha Hadid, it's an astonishing piece of architecture that resembles a giant silver spaceship that's landed in downtown Seoul. You can head inside to explore its fascinating interior with passageways leading to galleries, museums and exhibition halls. Be sure to visit archaeological remains at its attached Dongdaemun History Museum.

Best
Food

Sampling the varied and – to international travellers – generally unfamiliar delights of Korean cuisine is one of Seoul's great pleasures. Restaurants, cafes and street stalls are scattered throughout every neighbourhood with options to suit all budgets and tastes – from small, unpretentious joints serving healthy rice and vegetables or DIY barbecue, to the overflowing abundance and delicacy of a royal banquet.

WEX.WEX/GETTY IMAGES ©

Food Trends

While Korean food has been the darling of hipster food trends overseas for some years now, Seoul in turn has an obsession with international food. One current trend is Seoul's infatuation with American cuisine, where Southern-style barbecue, Maine lobster rolls and pulled-pork sandwiches are all the rage. Fusion food is another big hit, mixing traditional Korean flavours with contemporary dishes – from kimchi tacos at LA-style food trucks to high-end molecular fusion.

Korean Meals

A traditional Korean meal (either breakfast, lunch or dinner) typically consists of meat, seafood or fish served at the same time as soup, rice and a collection of dipping sauces and *banchan*, the ubiquitous cold side dishes. The fermented kimchi cabbage or radish is the most popular side dish, but there are many others, such as bean sprouts, black beans, dried anchovy, spinach, quail eggs, shellfish, lettuce, acorn jelly and tofu.

Street Food

Some of the best food you'll taste in Seoul is from stalls set up in market alleyways, street carts on main roads or late-night *pojangmacha* (plastic tent bars).

☑ **Top Tips**

▶ In Seoul, eating out is a group activity, and a number of Korean meals, such as *galbi* (beef ribs) or *jjimdak* (spicy chicken pieces with noodles), are not usually available for just one person.

▶ Korean barbecue dishes are served with lettuce and sesame leaves *(ssam)*; take a leaf and load it with meat and flavourings, and roll it up to eat it in one go.

Best Korean

Jungsik Neo-Korean fine dining at affordable prices. (p107)

Samwon Garden The classic *galbi* experience. (p106)

Korea House Traditional banquet and performance. (p62)

Tosokchon Ginseng chicken stew that's worth the long wait. (p38)

Gogung Jeonju-style bibimbap rice dishes. (p59)

Best International

GastroTong Sophisticated Swiss-European cuisine. (p40)

Linus' BBQ Alabama-style barbecue. (p89)

Ciuri Ciuri Savour Sicilian dishes in Hongdae. (p74)

Vatos Mexican street tacos with Korean flavours. (p88)

Tuk Tuk Noodle Thai Uncompromising flavours at a top Thai restaurant. (p73)

Samarkand Uzbekistan lamb shashliks and breads. (p122)

Best Cheap Eats

Tongin Market Box Lunch Café Old-school market arcade. (p38)

Tobang Great-value set Korean meals. (p29)

Myeong-dong Gyoja Hand-pulled noodle soup with dumplings. (p58)

Menya Sandaime Slurp up delicious bowls of ramen. (p67)

Best for Special Occasions

Congdu Subtle contemporary twists on Korean classics. (p38)

N.Grill Incredible views and French cuisine cooked by a Michelin-starred chef. (p60)

Min's Club Elegant Korea-meets-Europe experience for food and surroundings. (p39)

Best Markets

Noryangjin Fish Market Super-fresh fish dinners at Korea's largest seafood market. (p73)

Gwangjang Market Tasty and cheap street food in a covered market. (p122)

Namdaemun Market Food alleys serving bibimbap and noodle dishes. (p48)

Dongdaemun Market Street food and inexpensive eateries. (p122)

Best Vegetarian

Gosang Buddhist temple dishes dating from the Goryeo dynasty. (p60)

Balwoo Gongyang Buddhist vegetarian feasts overlooking Jogye-sa. (p39)

PLANT Vegan bakery and cafe in Itaewon. (p89)

Loving Hut Vegan haven in Sinchon. (p74)

Best Bakeries & Desserts

Passion 5 Glitzy arcade with gourmet foods. (p89)

Suji's Proper breakfasts and homebaked goods. (p91)

Fell & Cole Uniquely flavoured ice creams. (p67)

Best
Historical Sights

While centuries of invasion, war and fires have meant Seoul's 14th-century Joseon-dynasty palaces, city walls, gates and temples sites have all been painstakingly rebuilt countless times, you'll encounter many magnificent sights that show off the grandeur from the history of this era. Landmarks and architecture from its more recent colonial history can also be seen.

Palaces

During the Joseon era (1392–1897), five main palaces were constructed in the royal capital. These were cities unto themselves, massive complexes with administrative offices, residences, pleasure pavilions and royal gardens, all hemmed in by imposing walls.

Seoul City Wall & Gates

By the late 14th century an 18.6km wall encircled Seoul, linking up the peaks of Bukaksan (342m), Naksan (125m), Namsan (262m) and Inwangsan (338m) and punctuated by four major gates facing north, south, east and west. Over time parts of the wall were demolished and today only 10.5km of it remains. The city has been restoring some of the missing sections, and these are on view today.

Temples, Shrines & Tombs

Serene Buddhist temples and Confucian shrines are scattered around the city, offering respite from Seoul's high-rises and congested traffic. Also visually striking are the Unesco World Heritage–listed royal shrines and burial tombs of the Joseon dynasty found around Seoul.

Best Palaces

Gyeongbokgung The largest of Seoul's palaces, with museums and changing of the guard. (p24)

Changdeokgung The most attractive one, with a 'secret garden'. (p26)

Deoksugung A mix of architectural styles where Korea's last emperor lived. (p50; pictured above)

Gyeonghuigung Secondary palace of 10 Joseon-dynasty kings. (p36)

Changgyeonggung Has a beautiful pond and an elegant greenhouse. (p36)

Unhyeongung Here you can watch a traditional music performance on Fridays. (p36)

Best Hanok

Bukchon Hanok Village
A neighbourhood with
Seoul's highest concen-
tration of *hanok* (traditional wooden homes).
(p30)

**Namsangol Hanok
Village** Wonderful
display of aristocratic
houses that have been
relocated to this cultural
village. (p54)

Best for Gates,
Tombs &
City Walls

Seonjeongneung The
grassy mound tombs
of past Korean kings in
Seolleung Park. (p104)

Bongsudae These
500-year-old brick
signal beacons on top of
Namsan were used as a
communication system
to notify the govern-
ment of urgent matters.
(p47)

City Wall Some of the
most atmospheric sec-
tions of Seoul's original
walls snake across
Namsan. (p46)

Heunginjimun Seoul's
attractive 700-year-old
eastern gate looks as
grand as ever after re-
cent renovations. (p119)

Sungnyemun The
picturesque 14th-century
Great South Gate stands
opposite Namdaemun
Market. (p49)

Best Temples &
Shrines

Jongmyo Houses the
spirit tablets of the Jo-
seon kings and queens.
(p34)

Jogye-sa Home to
Daeungjeon, the largest
Buddhist temple building
in Seoul. (p28)

Bongeun-sa Attractive
Buddhist temple com-
plex with serene halls,

statues and gardens.
(p103)

Best for Modern
History

**Demilitarized Zone
(DMZ)** An enduring
remnant of the Korean
War, this heavily mili-
tarised border divides
North from South along
the Korean peninsula.
(p96)

**Jeoldusan Martyrs'
Shrine** Memorial
museum and church
dedicated to Korea's
Catholic martyrs and
saints. (p70)

Seoul Plaza Fronted
by a 1926 Renaissance-
style building, Seoul
Plaza has been the
gathering spot for mass
protests and celebra-
tions during the 20th
century. (p54)

Worth a Trip
Built in 1908, **Seodaemun Prison History Hall** (서대문형무소역사관;
www.sscmc.or.kr/culture2/foreign/eng/eng01.html; 251 Tongil-ro, Seodaemun-gu; adult/
child/youth ₩3000/100/1500; ⏰9.30am-6pm Tue-Sun Mar-Oct, to 5pm Tue-Sun Nov-Feb;
⑤Line 3 to Dongnimmun, Exit 5) is a symbol of Japanese cruelty and oppression
during its rule of Korea from 1910 to 1945. It was also used by Korea's various
postwar dictators until its closure in 1987. View the original cell blocks where
inmates were held.

Best
Drinking & Nightlife

MULTI-BITS/GETTY IMAGES ©

From quaintly rustic teahouses and coffee roasters to craft beer pubs and classy cocktail bars, Seoul offers an unbelievable number of places to relax over a drink. No-frills *hof* (pubs) are common, and don't miss that quintessential Seoul nightlife experience: *soju* (vodka) shots and snacks at a *pojangmacha* (street tent bar). Save yourself for a late night out clubbing, particularly in Gangnam, which is home to many megaclubs.

Craft Beer

At the epicentre of the craft beer revolution in Seoul, Noksapyeong (in Gyeongridan up from Itaewon) is home to a string of brewers who have set up shop in what's now known locally as Craft Beer Valley. In just a few years, this localised scene has paved the way for a greater diversity and quality of beer, resulting in a shift in tastes that's seen locals gain a thirst for IPAs, amber ales, German-style wheat beers and smokey stouts.

Traditional Korean Alcohol

Makgeolli – a milky alcoholic brew made from unrefined, fermented rice, and long popular among the older generation – is catching on with the young and trendy, too. Seoul has several bars now where higher-quality styles of *makgeolli,* akin to the range of Japanese sake, are served and savoured.

☑ **Top Tip**

▶ For those interested in traditional Korean liquors, get in touch with appreciation groups **Makgeolli Mamas & Papas** (MMPKorea; http://mmpkorea. wordpress.com) and **Makgeolli Makers** (www.face book.com/makgeolli makers; Susubori Academy, 47 Kyonggidae-ro, Seodaemun-gu; course ₩45,000; [S] Line 2 or 5 to Chungjeongno, Exit 7). The latter can teach you how to brew your own batch.

Best for Traditional Alcohol

Baekseju-maeul *Makgeolli* bar run by craft brewers, Kooksoondang. (p40)

Damotori A cherished local, specialising in *makgeolli*. (p84)

Neurin Maeul Craft *makgeolli* and *soju* bar by Baesangmyeon Brewery. (p108)

Wolhyang Casual joint for sampling *makgeolli* in Hongdae and Itaewon. (p75)

Story of the Blue Star Brass kettles full of *makgeolli* served in a divey hang-out. (p40)

Moon Jar Smart and rustic bar with a good menu. (p108)

Best for Clubbing

Club Octagon Regarded as one of the world's best. (p107)

Ellui Another famous Gangnam megaclub. (p109)

Cakeshop Fun-lovin', divey club in Itaewon. (p85)

M2 Huge underground space for parties in Hongdae. (p77)

Best Cafes/Bars

Anthracite Top independent coffee-roaster and cafe in happening Sangsu. (p75)

Sik Mool Sophisticated *hanok* cafe-bar in up-and-coming Ikseon-dong. (p40)

Steamers Coffee Factory Third-wave coffee-roasting champs. (p108)

Café Sukkara Rustic and lovely; on the edge of Hongdae. (p76)

Best for Craft Beer

Craftworks Responsible for kicking off Seoul's craft beer scene. (p60)

Magpie Brewing Co One of Seoul's originals with branches in Gyeongridan and Hongdae. (p85)

Pongdang Korean brewer that knows its stuff. (p108)

Booth Another big player, with brewpubs across the city. (p108)

Best for Cocktails

Southside Parlor Artisan cocktails by hipster mixologists. (p85)

Flower Gin Intimate gin bar that doubles as a florist. (p85)

Best Teahouses

Dawon Traditional teahouse in the heart of Insa-dong set around a spacious courtyard. (p40)

Cha Masineun Tteul Enjoy steamed pumpkin cake and lovely views. (p31)

Worth a Trip
Based in a 1930s *hanok* that was once the home of novelist Lee Tae-jun, **Suyeon Sanbang** (수연 산방; 8 Seongbuk-ro 26-gil, Seongbuk-gu; 11.30am-10pm; Line 4 to Hangsung University, Exit 6 then 1111, 2112) is Seoul's most charming teahouse. Apart from a range of medicinal teas and premium quality wild green tea, it also serves traditional sweets.

Best
Architecture

ANDRÉS GUERRERO COLLADO/GETTY IMAGES ©

Seoul's skyline – dominated by skyscrapers – suggests no building has survived the war and economic modernisation. But architecture from all periods of Seoul's history does remain. Visitors will discover not only city walls, grand palaces and decorative temples, but also charming *hanok* (traditional wooden homes) and dramatic contemporary structures.

Modern Architecture

Over the last decade Seoul has worked hard to soften its industrial hard edges into an appealing urban ideal of parks, culture and design. Glass, concrete and steel are crafted into natural forms at the spectacular Dongdaemun Design Plaza & Park and the new City Hall.

Traditional Architecture

There are three main types of traditional architecture found in Seoul: palaces, temples and homes. They are all primarily made of wood, with no nails used – a system of braces and brackets holds the elements together. A prominent feature is the roof of these structures, which is made from heavy clay tiles with dragons or other mythical beasts embossed on the end tile. The strikingly bold, predominantly green-and-orange paintwork under the eaves is called *dancheong*.

Hanok

These one-storey homes are complex in design yet masterfully understated. They are crafted entirely from wood, save for the clay-tiled roofs, while the windows are made of a thin paper that allows daylight to stream in. They're insulated with mud and straw, and heated by the underfloor system called *ondol*.

Best Colonial Architecture

Seoul Metropolitan Library The former City Hall, this 1926 Renaissance-style building is fronted by its iconic analogue clock. (p54)

Deoksugung Among the traditional Korean halls and pavilions are neo-classical 20th-century architecture by British, Japanese and Russian architects. (p50)

Myeong-dong Catholic Cathedral Gothic-style cathedral with a vaulted ceiling and stained-glass windows. (p56)

Culture Station Seoul 284 The former Seoul station with domed roof dates from 1925. (p55)

Bank of Korea Money Museum Attractive Japanese colonial building dating from 1912. (p56)

Ewha Womans University (p70)

Seoul Museum of Art A grand building that dates from 1928 and was the former Supreme Court. (p55)

Best Joseon-Era Architecture

Gyeongbokgung The largest of Seoul's palaces, fronted by a grand gateway. (p24)

Changdeokgung Features its beautiful main palace, Injeongjeon. (p26)

Jongmyo One of Seoul's best-preserved Confucian shrines and World Heritage–listed. (p34)

Sungnyemun The recently restored South Gate is an imposing sight rising above the traffic. (p49)

Best Contemporary Architecture

Dongdaemun Design Plaza & Park Zaha Hadid's sleek silvery landmark is straight out of a sci-fi fantasy. (p116)

Some Sevit These futuristic buildings sit on three artificial islands on the Han River and glow bright at night. (p103)

Seoul City Hall This giant glass wave is a modern reinterpretation of traditional Korean design. (p54)

Ewha Womans University Dominique Perrault's stunning main entrance dives six storeys underground. (p70)

Best Landmarks

N Seoul Tower Seoul's most iconic structure sits atop Namsan. (p46)

Lotte World Tower Set to be the peninsula's tallest building, this 555m-high tower was inspired by traditonal Korean ceramics. (p105)

63 Square One of Seoul's tallest buildings, this gleaming skyscraper has a 60th-floor observation deck offering panoramic views. (p72)

Best Hanok

Namsangol Hanok Village Five differing *yangban* (upper-class) houses are in this park at the foot of Namsan. (p54)

Bukchon Hanok Village Around 900 *hanok* are found in this traditional neighbourhood. (p30)

Best
Museums & Galleries

The standard of museums in Seoul is world-class, often superbly presented within elegant buildings. They cover varied subject matter from Korean history – from the dynasties of the Three Kingdoms – to traditional music and culture, and more recent events such as the Korean War, with engaging exhibits. Art galleries are another huge highlight. Contemporary galleries abound, from small-scale exhibitions to chic private galleries to internationally renowned art museums.

WIBOWO RUSLI/GETTY IMAGES ©

☑ **Top Tip**

▶ On the last Wednesday of each month, many museums and galleries (as well as cultural sites) can be visited free of charge.

Best for Traditional Korean History

National Museum of Korea Packed with national treasures spanning the centuries. (p82)

Museum of Gugak Interesting selction of traditional Korean stringed instruments and drums, including some you can play. (p105)

Seoul City Wall Museum Multimedia displays and artefacts that cover the history of the 14th-century wall that encloses the city. (p119)

Dongdaemun History Museum Displays of relics dating from the Joseon dynasty unearthed during excavations of Dongdaemun Design Plaza & Park. (p117)

National Folk Museum of Korea Fascinating exhibits indoors and in the palace grounds. (p25)

Best for Modern History

War Memorial & Museum Masses of military-related displays and good exhibits on the Korean War. (p88)

Seoul Museum of History Learn how much the city has changed over the last century. (p35)

National Museum of Korean Contemporary History Walk through a visual record of the country's recent past. (p35)

Cheonggyecheon Museum Interesting overview of the resurrection

of this beloved central city watercourse. (p119)

War & Women's Human Rights Museum Sombre account of suffering endured by Korean 'comfort women' under Japanese occupation. (p70)

Daehan Empire History Museum Glimpse the lavish lifestyle of Joseon royalty within this magnificent 20th-century building. (p51)

Best for Contemporary Art

Leeum Samsung Museum of Art Top

War Memorial of Korea (p88)

architect-designed buildings and a stunning collection of art. (p88)

MMCA Seoul The new city centre branch of the National Museum of Contemporary Art; with the main branch in Seoul Grand Park. (p36)

Arario Museum in SPACE Part of an amazing private collection in a sleekly converted iconic 1970s building. (p34)

PLATEAU Notable for its Rodin sculptures and quality art shows. (p56)

SOMA Sleek gallery in Olympic Park. (p113)

Seoul Museum of Art Excellent contemporary art in the former Supreme Court building. (p55)

Culture Station Seoul 284 Regular exhibitions in the former Seoul station building. (p55)

Arko Art Centre Avant-garde art shows over multiple galleries. (p43)

313 Art Project Small gallery that packs a punch with local and international exhibitions. (p101)

Best of the Rest

Bank of Korea Money Museum All about currency, with interactive features. (p56)

Modern Design Museum Fascinating private collection on modern design in Korea. (p71)

Lock Museum Exhibits locks as both lovely works of art and fearsome apparatus, such as a medieval chastity belt. (p43)

Seoul Yangnyeongsi Herb Medicine Museum Learn about your yin, yang and *sasang* (traditional medicine). (p125)

Worth a Trip

Featuring the work of internationally acclaimed avant-garde artist Nam June Paik (1932–2006), the **Nam June Paik Art Center** (031-201 8500; http://njpac-en. ggcf.kr; 10 Paiknam-june-ro, Giheung-gu, Yongin-si; admission ₩4000; 10am-6pm) shows a changing collection of his pioneering new-media work, namely his signature TV sets. From Seoul take the subway on Budang Line to Sanggal Station, from where it's a 10-minute walk.

Best
Entertainment

Best for Theatre & Dance

National Gugak Center Traditional Korean classical music and folk music and dance. (p109)

Seoul Arts Centre Opera, concert and recital performances. (p110)

Nanta The first and the best of Seoul's wide selection of nonverbal shows. (p61)

National Theatre of Korea Home to the national drama, *changgeuk* (Korean opera), orchestra and dance companies. (p62)

Sejong Centre for the Performing Arts Big musicals and intimate classical concerts are staged here. (p41)

ArkoPAC Theatre company that specialises in dance performances. (p43)

Best for K-Indie

Thunderhorse Tavern Divey Itaewon venue hosting local and expat bands. (p93)

FF Come early to hear local indie bands banging out their sets. (p78)

DGBD Standing room only at this legendary rock venue. (p67)

Club Ta Hub of Hongdae's ska and ska-punk scene. (p78)

Best for Jazz

All That Jazz Long-established, well-respected Itaewon venue. (p93)

Once in a Blue Moon Stylish bar with quality performers. (p110)

Club Evans Evergreen Hongdae jazz haunt. (p77)

Best Mixed Events

Mudaeruk Electronica, films and art in the basement of the Lost Continent of Mu. (p77)

Café BBang Indie artists and bands as well as film, art exhibitions and parties. (p78)

Indie Art-Hall GONG All kinds of cool goings on in part of a steel factory south of the Han. (p78)

JORDAN PIX/CONTRIBUTOR/GETTY IMAGES ©

☑ **Top Tip**

▶ Baseball games take place at Jamsil Baseball Stadium (p110) from April to October, with a lively boozy atmosphere and plenty of off-field entertainment. Games generally start at 6.30pm.

Best for K-Pop

Klive Hologram concert by hottest K-Pop stars. (p123)

K-Wave Experience Get the full K-Pop makeover and photo op. (p101)

Seoul Global Cultural Center K-Pop dance classes to learn all the latest moves. (p56)

K-Star Road Take a stroll down the 'Hallyuwood' Walk of Fame. (p100)

Best
Gay & Lesbian

Korea is a sexually conservative society and although the country has never outlawed homosexuality, this shouldn't be taken as a sign of tolerance or acceptance. Attitudes are changing, especially among young people, but virtually all of the local gay population (called *ivan* in Korean) chooses to stay firmly in the closet.

GLBT-Friendly Areas

These areas include Itaewon (mainly gay and transsexual/transvestite bars), Nagwon-dong and Dongui-dong near Insa-dong (gay bars), and Hongdae and Edae (mainly lesbian bars). Itaewon is the main area for GLBT foreign travellers, with 'Homo Hill' (p92) being famous for its cluster of gay-friendly bars and clubs. There are also scores of GLBT-run bars around Jongno 3-ga subway station; however, not all welcome foreigners, and some levy a hefty cover charge for *anju* (snacks). Alternatively, the outdoor *pojangmacha* (street tent bars) around Jongno 3-ga, offering cheap beer, *soju* (vodka) and snacks, are prime gay hang-outs.

Best Bars

Queen (www.facebook.com/queenbar; 7, Usadan-ro 12-gil; ⏱8pm-5am Tue-Sun; Ⓢ Line 6 to Itaewon, Exit 3) Popular bar on Itaewon's 'Homo Hill'.

Always Homme (올웨이즈옴므; www.facebook.com/AlwaysHommeBar; Usadan-ro 12-gil; ⏱8pm-4am Sun-Thu, to 6am Fri & Sat; Ⓢ Line 6 to Itaewon, Exit 3)

Friendly and fun lounge bar that's a perennial Itaewon favourite.

Best Lesbian Bars

Labris (라브리스; 📞02-333 5276; 81-Wausan-ro, Map-gu; ⏱7pm-2am Mon-Thu, to 5am Fri-Sun; Ⓢ Line 6 to Sangsu, Exit 1) Not exclusively lesbian, this women-only bar has DJs on weekends.

SERTS/GETTY IMAGES ©

☑ Top Tip

▶ In mid-June, Seoul pins up its rainbow colours for the Korea Queer Festival.

Miracle (Usadan-ro; ⏱8pm-5am; Ⓢ Line 6 to Itaewon, Exit 3) Intimate bar at the top of 'Homo Hill'.

Best Clubs

Trance (http://cafe.daum.net/trance; Usadan-ro; admission incl 1 drink ₩10,000; ⏱10.30pm-5am; Ⓢ Line 6 to Itaewon, Exit 3) Drag queens and DJs.

Club MWG (www.facebook.com/clubmwg1; 6-5, Wausan-ro 19-gil, Mapo-gu; ⏱10pm-5am Fri & Sat; Ⓢ Line 2 to Hongik University, Exit 2) Grungy Hongdae club hosting regular GLBT events.

Best
Shopping

Whether it's with traditional items such as *hanbok* (clothing) or *hanji* (handmade paper), art-and-design pieces, digital gizmos or K-Pop CDs, chances are slim that you will leave Seoul empty-handed. The city's teeming markets, electronics emporia, underground arcades, upmarket department stores and glitzy malls are all bursting at the seams with more goodies than Santa's sack.

STEVE VIDLER/GETTY IMAGES ©

☑ Top Tip

▶ At Namdaemun Market, the wholesale handicrafts market in Buildings C and D also has traditional Korean cookware such as stone bowls, cutlery and tea cups.

Markets

One of the highlights of Seoul is undoubtedly throwing yourself into the fray and joining the masses in one of its hectic markets. From food alleys at traditional arcade markets to more cruisy weekend art and craft markets, there's a good variation of experiences to be had.

Times vary, but some stalls may stay open even on days when a market is generally closed.

Best Handicrafts & Souvenirs

KCDF Gallery Gorgeous design emporium embracing traditional crafts with a contemporary slant. (p41)

Insa-dong Maru Slick showcase for local crafts, fashion and homewares. (p41)

Eelskin Shop Nab a unique souvenir with accessories made from ultrasoft skin from eels. (p95)

Namdaemun Market Folk art, handicrafts and *hanbok*. (p48)

Dongjin Market A hipster magnet with its second-hand clothing and homemade items. (p74)

Stairway Flea Market Set up by local artists, this cool little market takes place on a steep staircase near Itaewon's mosque. (p95)

Free Market Indie weekend market with stalls selling cool crafts. (p78)

Best Department Stores

COEX Mall A shiny, modern megamall that's Asia's largest underground shopping precinct. (p111)

Lotte Department Store Several branches across the city, including its original colossus shopping precinct. (p63)

Shinsegae The 'Harrods' of Seoul is the city's classiest department store. (p62)

COEX Mall (p111)

Galleria Haute couture along Apgujeong Rodeo St. (p100)

Best Fashion

Lab 5 Good spot to seek out the latest in K-design. (p63)

10 Corso Como Seoul Beautifully curated high-fashion and lifestyle store in Cheongdam. (p110)

Doota Buzzing fashion mall with domestic brands, luxury designers and accessories. (p124)

Åland Excellent selection of street wear for men and women. (p63)

Jilkyungyee Tastefully designed *hanbok* for both sexes. (p31)

Gentle Monster Edgy shades as worn by Korean stars. (p79)

Best Vintage & Secondhand

Seoul Folk Flea Market Old vinyl, watches, military paraphernalia and retro electronics, it's all here. (p124)

Gwangjang Market Expansive upstairs vintage clothes market with plenty of cool stuff. (p124)

Yongsan Electronics Market Sprawling complex with all the latest digital gadgets, as well as secondhand smart phones. (p95)

Dapsimni Antiques Market Centuries-old antiques for the serious collector. (p125)

Best Traditional Markets

Gwangjang Market Most famous for food, but also has vintage clothing and textiles. (p124)

Namdaemun Market Korea's largest and most atmospheric market. (p48)

Dongdaemun Market Energetic 24-hour shopping and a good market for food. (p124)

Jungang Market One of Seoul's oldest arcade markets offers a more local experience. (p124)

Seoul Yangnyeongsi Herb Medicine Market Take in wonderful fragrances at Asia's largest herbal market. (p125)

Best
Parks & Gardens

For one of the world's most populated, modern cities, Seoul has an impressive amount of green space. Hike one of its nearby mountains, admire a traditional 14th-century garden or get lost in an inner-city forest.

NMT PHOTOGRAPHY/GETTY IMAGES ©

Best Gardens

Changdeokgung Beautiful World Heritage–listed 15th-century palace with serene traditional garden. (p26; pictured right)

National Museum of Korea The adjoining wooded Yongsan Park is full of trees, ponds, pavilions and many species of bird. (p82)

Best Green Spaces

Seoul Forest Expansive park by the Han River with wetlands and sika deer. (p121)

World Cup Park Comprising five parks that were formerly landfill, it has plenty of walking and cycling paths. (p71)

Seonjeongneung Park Large inner-city grassy enclosure that houses the tombs of two Korean

kings and one queen. (p104)

Seonyudo Park Beautiful park and gardens on an island in the Han River. (p72)

Olympic Park Home to a 1700-year-old earth fort and over 200 quirky sculptures. (p113)

Best Walks

Namsan The mountain at the heart of the city, criss-crossed with hiking trails and walking paths. (p46)

Naksan Park Heading east, the lowest of the guardian mountains with the arty neighbourhood of Ihwa-dong on its slopes. (p43)

Best Urban Parks

Skygarden New project that will redevelop a highway overpass into

☑ Top Tips

▶ To visit Huwon 'secret garden' at Changdeokgun you need to visit on a tour; book online or come early, as the Huwon tours are restricted to 50 people at a time.

▶ Seoul Forest is big, so hire a bike from the rental stall to see it all.

a elevated park similar to New York's High Line. (p56)

Cheong-gye-cheon The long-buried central city stream now sparkles in the light of day. (p34)

Best
With Kids

Children are welcomed in Seoul – this is a safe and family-friendly city with plenty of interesting museums (including several devoted to kids themselves), as well as parks, amusement parks and fun events that will appeal to all age groups.

MASTAPIECE/SHUTTERSTOCK ©

Best Museums

National Museum of Korea Has an interactive children's museum that's a lot of fun. (p82)

National Children's Museum A hands-on museum that allows kids to learn about Korean culture. (p25)

War Memorial & Museum Plenty of kid-friendly exhibitions such as 4D movies and other fun stuff. (p88)

Best Parks

Lotte World Popular amusement park with indoor fantasy land and outdoor adventure thrills. (p103)

Children's Grand Park This giant park covers everything from theme parks and a zoo to playgrounds. (p119)

Seoul Forest Hire a kid's bike to pedal around this lovely parkland, with deer and butterfly enclosures. (p121)

Olympic Park Massive parkland in which to run around and feed the ducks. (p113)

Best of the Rest

Klive Virtual reality K-Pop concert with holograms. (p123)

K-Wave Experience Dress up as a K-Pop star for a photo op. (p101)

Seoul Global Cultural Center Dress up in traditional clothes, take handicraft lessons or K-Pop dance classes. (p56)

COEX Aquarium Giant underwater world with sharks, piranhas and electric eels. (p106)

 **Top Tips**

▶ A few top hotels and residences can arrange babysitting.

▶ The mammoth **Everland** (www.everland.com) amusement park, 40km south of Seoul, is regarded as Korea's best. Only 50 minutes by bus, it's an easy half-day trip.

Banpo Bridge Rainbow Fountain Colourful spectacle held nightly on the Han River. (p103)

Bau House Dog-themed cafe to play with pooches. (p76)

TableA Cuddle cats and kittens to your heart's content. (p76)

Best
For Free

MARTIN ROBINSON/GETTY IMAGES ©

There's plenty to see and do in Seoul without breaking the bank. Admission to most royal palaces is not costly and usually includes free guided tours. Additionally, it costs nothing to enjoy the changing-of-the-guard ceremonies at Gyeongbokgung and Deoksugung. You can also view aristocratic *hanok* (traditional wooden homes) for free in Bukchon, Seochon and Ikseon-dong. The list of museums with free entry is extensive.

Public Art

There are thousands of interesting outdoor sculptures scattered across Seoul, with over 200 of them alone in Olympic Park. And for fun, inventive street art, wander the alleys of Ihwa-dong and Mullae Arts Village. You don't need to be a buyer to drop by the scores of free art-gallery shows in areas such as Insa-dong and Samcheong-dong.

Outdoors

Legions of locals take full advantage of Seoul's mountainous topography. All four of the city's guardian mountains – Bukaksan, Naksan, Namsan and Inwangsan – have hiking routes; the really keen can summit them all by following the remains of the Seoul City Wall. The free panoramic city views are your reward for the effort.

Festivals

Not a week goes by without a free festival or event happening somewhere in the city. Seoul's government often puts on free shows in Seoul Plaza in front of City Hall, and there's the spectacular lighting up of the fountain flowing off Banpo Bridge in the warmer months.

Best Free Palaces & Temples

Gyeonghuigung A 17th-century palace with lovely audience hall. (p36)

Jogye-sa Seoul's largest Buddhist worship hall. (p28)

Bongeun-sa Beautiful Buddhist temple is a sanctuary from city life. (p103)

Best Free Performances

Marronnier Park Regular free performances held in the afternoons and evenings on its outdoor stage. (p43; pictured above)

Seoul Plaza Seoul's government often puts on free shows in summer. (p54)

Banpo Bridge Rainbow Fountain (p103)

Best Museums & Galleries

National Museum of Korea The country's best history museum is also free, and includes English tours. (p82)

War Memorial & Museum Exceptional museum that covers the Korean War, with state-of-the-art exhibits. (p88)

National Museum of Korean Contemporary History Interesting coverage of more recent events that have shaped modern Seoul. (p35)

Seoul Museum of History Exhibits cover Seoul's history from the Joseon dynasty to the 20th century. (p35)

Seoul Museum of Art World-class art museum in an attractive colonial building. (p55)

Best for Architecture

Seoul City Hall & Library Interesting contrast of contemporary and historic styles. (p54)

Dongdaemun Design Plaza Cutting-edge sci-fi architecture with many free exhibtions within. (p116)

Some Sevit & Rainbow Fountain Contemporary buildings illuminated at night, along with the Banpo Bridge Rainbow Fountain show. (p103)

Best in Culture

Namsangol Hanok Village Traditional architecture as well as free performances such a taekwondo displays. (p54)

Bukchon Traditional Culture Center Get a lowdown on the neighbourhood before visiting its *hanok*. (p30)

Seoul Global Cultural Center Offers a range of free activities such as traditional craft lessons or dressing in *hanbok*. (p56)

K-Wave Experience A fun stop to dress up as a K-Pop star. (p101)

Best
Art & Design

Seoul has a thriving contemporary-art scene, with local artists incorporating Korean motifs and themes, and sometimes traditional techniques, with a modern vision. Insa-dong, Bukchon, Samcheong-dong and Tongui-dong are all packed with small galleries, often with free shows; you'll also find major galleries south of the river in Cheongdam. Dongdaemun Design Plaza also hosts regular design exhibitions, markets and fairs.

Street Art
There's a particularly healthy street-art scene in Hongdae near Hongik University subway (exit 4) with its backstreets and alleys full of cool stencils, murals, graffiti and paste-ups. Mullae Arts Village and HBC Art Village also have plenty of urban art to check out. You'll find several mural villages where artists are commissioned to beautify gritty neighbourhoods too, the most well known is Ihwa Maeul.

Multiperformance
Seoul has a lively multiperformance-art scene. **Crazy Multiply** (www.crazymultiply.com) puts on monthly shows that combine music, art and performance art. The annual Festival Bo:m, which showcases dance, theatre, art, music and film, is also worth checking out in March.

Best for Street Art
Ihwa Maeul Downtrodden neighbourhood that's undergone transformation. (p43)

Mullae Arts Village Go on a street-art safari around the small metalwork factories. (p70)

Best for Art & Craft
Free Market Weekly creative market in Hongdae. (p78)

HBC Art Village Newish art project with murals and street art commissioned in Haebangchon's backstreets. (p95)

T. DALLAS/SHUTTERSTOCK ©

Dongjin Market Saturday craft and secondhand-clothes market. (p78)

Best Art & Design
KT&G SangsangMadang Mix of galleries devoted to experimental, fringe exhibitions, with a great design shop for gifts on the ground floor. (p67)

Seoul Art Space Sindang Artists and designers have set up studios and shops in this arcade beneath Jungang Market. (p119)

Seoul Arts Space – Mullae Gallery and studio spaces. (p70)

Indie Art-Hall GONG Large art space covers visual and performance-art shows. (p78)

Citizens Hall Mix of cutting-edge multimedia art exhibitions and design shops. (p54)

Survival Guide

Survival Guide

Before You Go

When to Go

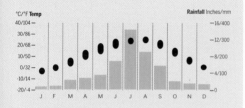

°C/°F Temp
Rainfall Inches/mm

→ Winter (Dec–Feb)
Cosy *ondol* (underfloor) heating and public ice-skating rinks, but bitterly cold temperatures.

→ Spring (Mar–Apr)
Peak season to visit, with sunny weather, cherry blossoms and top events such as Jongmyo Daeje and Lotus Lantern Festival.

→ Summer (May–Aug)
Sweltering, muggy and often rainy weather; a good time to take a plunge in Han River swimming pools.

→ Autumn (Sep–Nov)
Prime time to visit with mild weather and excellent hiking across mountains coated in brilliant colours.

Book Your Stay

☑ **Top Tip** Traditional *hanok* (wooden houses) offer a unique and memorable experience; some offer cultural programs such as dressing in *hanbok* (traditional Korean clothing) or cooking classes.

→ Backpacker guesthouses are mostly concentrated around Myeong-dong, Itaewon and Hongdae.

→ Love motels cater for couples seeking some by-the-hour privacy, but they also accept conventional overnight guests. They can be excellent value, with facilities not dissimilar to top-end hotels.

Useful Websites

Lonely Planet (www.hotels.lonelyplanet.com) Bookings for all kinds of accommodation in Seoul.

Korean Hotel Reservation Center (www.khrc.com) Check for low rates on top-end hotels.

Koreastay (www.koreastay.
r.kr) Booking site run
by the Korean Tourism
Organization.

Homestay Korea (www.
homestaykorea.com) If
you wish to stay with a
Korean family.

Hanok Homestay
(http://homestay.jongno.
go.kr/homestayEngMain.
do) Family homestay
program.

Best Budget

Itaewon G Guest House
(www.gguest.com) Grungy
apartment block con-
verted to cool backpack-
ers, with a sensational
rooftop hang-out.

Urbanwood Guesthouse
(www.urbanwood.co.kr) Cool,
colourful apartment
living in the heart of
Hongdae.

K Hostel (www.khostel.
net) Vibrant backpackers
full of murals with a cool
rooftop.

Doo Guesthouse (www.
dooguesthouse.com) Best
of the budget *hanok*
guesthouses.

Best Midrange

**Hide & Seek Guest-
house** (www.hidenseek.
co.kr) Worth tracking

down this gem near
Gyeongbokgung.

Minari House (www.
minarihouse.com) Creative,
arty base at the foot of
Ihwa-dong.

Small House Big Door
(www.smallhousebigdoor.
com) Art hotel in
downtown Seoul full of
designer touches.

Hotel Sunbee (www.
hotelsunbee.com) Huge
double beds in tastefully
decorated rooms.

Best Top End

Park Hyatt Seoul (www.
seoul.park.hyatt.com)
Sophisticated contem-
porary design hotel
overlooking COEX.

Grand Hyatt Seoul (www.
seoul.grand.hyatt.com) Ooz-
ing class on the hillside
of Namsan overlooking
Itaewon.

Plaza (www.hotel
theplaza.com) Large
rooms look down upon
grassy Seoul Plaza
and its historic-meets-
contemporary facade of
City Hall.

La Casa (www.hotellacasa.
kr) Chic boutique hotel
close to the trendy cafes
and bars of Garosu-gil.

Arriving in Seoul

☑ **Top Tip** For the best
way to get to your accom-
modation, see p17.

Incheon International Airport

The main international
gateway is **Incheon
International Airport**
(📞 02-1577 2600; www.
airport.kr; 🛜), 52km west
of central Seoul on the
island of Yeongjongdo.

➡ Two types of **A'REX**
(www.arex.or.kr) trains run
from the airport to Seoul
station. The express
train costs ₩14,300 (43
minutes) departing every
30 minutes (promo rates
₩8000). More frequent
commuter trains cost
₩4150 (53 minutes),
running between 5.20am
to 11.45pm.

➡ The city limousine bus-
es take an hour to reach
central Seoul (₩9000,
5.30am to 10pm, every
10 to 30 minutes). The
deluxe **KAL limousine
buses** (www.kallimousine.
com; ₩14,000) run along
four routes (₩14,000),
dropping passengers at
top hotels around Seoul.

→ Regular taxis charge around ₩60,000 to ₩100,000 for the 70-minute journey to downtown Seoul. From midnight to 4am there's a 20% surcharge.

Gimpo International Airport

Most domestic flights (and a handful of international ones) arrive at **Gimpo International Airport** (☎02-1661 2626; gimpo.airport.co.kr; West Seoul), 18km west of the city centre.

→ Subway lines 5 and 9 connect the airport with the city (₩1250, 35 minutes).

→ A'REX trains run to Seoul Station (₩1450, 15 minutes).

→ City/KAL limousine buses run every 10 minutes to central Seoul (from ₩5000/7000, around 40 minutes).

→ Taxis cost around ₩35,000 to the city centre and take around 40 minutes.

Getting Around

Subway

☑ **Best for...** getting around quickly, easily and cheaply.

→ Seoul has an excellent, user-friendly **subway system** (www.smrt.co.kr)

that connects destinations around the city and beyond, including Suwon and Incheon.

→ First train is 5.30am, and last around midnight (or earlier).

→ The minimum fare of ₩1300 (₩1250 with a T-Money card) takes you up to 12km.

→ The average time between stations is just over two minutes; with departures every five to 10 minutes.

→ Neighbourhood maps, including ones with digital touch screens, inside the stations help you figure out which subway exits to take.

Taxi

☑ **Best for...** short trips, groups of four, late-night commutes.

→ Regular orange- or grey-coloured taxis are a good deal for short trips.

→ The flagfall for 2km is ₩3000 and rises ₩100 for every 144m or 35 seconds after that if the taxi is travelling below 15km/h.

→ A 20% surcharge is levied between midnight and 4am.

→ Few taxi drivers speak English, but most taxis

Travel Passes & Tickets

Bus, subway, taxi and train fares can all be paid using the rechargeable touch-and-go **T-Money card** (http://eng.t-money.co.kr), which gives you a ₩100 discount per trip. The basic card can be bought for a nonrefundable ₩2500 at any subway station booth, bus kiosk and convenience store displaying the T-Money logo; reload it with credit at any of the aforementioned places, and get unused money (up to ₩20,000 minus a processing fee of ₩500) refunded at subway machines and participating convenience stores before you leave Seoul.

have a free interpretation service whereby an interpreter talks to the taxi driver and to you by phone.

➡ Orange **International Taxi** (📞 02-1644 2255; www.internationaltaxi.co.kr) has English-speaking drivers; these taxis can be reserved in advance for 20% extra on the regular fare and can be chartered on an hourly or daily basis for longer journeys.

Bus

☑ **Best for...** local experience, seeing the city.

➡ Seoul has a comprehensive and reasonably priced **bus system** (www.bus.go.kr; 🕐 5.30am-midnight).

➡ Using a T-Money card allows free transfers between the bus and subway. Put your card to the screen as you exit as well as when you get on a bus, just as you do on the subway.

➡ **Red buses** Long-distance express buses run to the outer suburbs.

➡ **Green buses** Link subways within a district.

➡ **Blue buses** Run to outer suburbs.

➡ **Yellow buses** Short-haul buses that circle small districts.

Bicycle

☑ **Best for...** scenic rides along the Han River.

➡ Bicycles can be rented (₩3000 per hour) at several parks along the Han River, including on Yeouido and at Seoul Forest Park. There's also free bicycle rental from designated subway stations, including Jamsil.

➡ Cycling the busy main streets of the city is not recommended.

Car & Motorcycle

☑ **Best for...** independence.

➡ Due to the traffic jams, the impatience and recklessness of other drivers, and lack of signs and parking, we recommend first-time visitors to Seoul give driving a miss.

➡ Driving is on the right.

➡ To rent a car, you must be over 21 and have both a driving licence from your own country and an International Driving Permit.

➡ Incheon International Airport has a couple of car-rental agencies. Try **KT Kumho** (📞 02-797 8000; www.ktkumhorent. com) or **Avis** (📞 032 743 3300; www.avis.com; Incheon

International Airport). Daily rates start at ₩80,000.

Essential Information

Business Hours

Banks 9am to 4pm Monday to Friday, ATMs 7am to 11pm

Bars 6pm to 1am, longer hours Friday and Saturday

Cafes 7am to 10pm

Post offices 9am to 6pm Monday to Friday

Restaurants 11am to 10pm

Shops 10am to 8pm

Discount Cards

Korea Pass (http://www.lottecard.co.kr/app/html/koreapass/IHKPAZZ_V100.jsp) is a prepaid card, available in denominations from ₩50,000 to ₩500,000, that provides discounts on a range of goods and services. It can be bought at Lotte Mart and conveniences stores in Seoul as well as the A'REX booth at Incheon International Airport.

Electricity

South Korea is on the 220V standard at 60Hz and uses two round pins with no earth.

220V/60Hz

220V/60Hz

Emergencies

If no English-speaking staff are available, ring the 24-hour tourist information and help line ☎1330.

→ **Ambulance** ☎119

→ **Fire Brigade** ☎119

→ **Police** ☎112

Internet Access

→ Wi-fi is universal and commonly free. Nearly all hotels offer it, too, for free.

→ The major phone companies offer modem devices to rent that connect to the internet anywhere around Korea.

Money

The South Korean unit of currency is the won (₩), with ₩10, ₩50, ₩100 and ₩500 coins. Notes come in denominations of ₩1000, ₩5000, ₩10,000 and ₩50,000.

See www.xe.com for up-to-date exchange rates.

ATMs

ATMs that accept foreign cards are common: look for ones that have a 'Global' sign or the logo of your credit-card company. ATMs often operate only from 7am to 11pm, but some are open 24

hours. Restrictions on the amount you can withdraw vary. It can be as low as ₩100,000 per day.

Changing Money

Many banks in Seoul offer a foreign-exchange service. There are also licensed moneychangers, particularly in Itaewon that keep longer hours than the banks and provide a faster service, but may only exchange US dollars cash.

Credit Cards

Hotels, shops and restaurants accept foreign credit cards, but plenty of places including budget accommodation and stalls require cash.

Money-Saving Tips

→ Make the most of free sights and entertainment.

→ If you spend more than ₩30,000 at participating tax-free shops, you can receive a partial refund on some items; be sure to collect the special receipt, and collect the refund from Incheon International Airport.

Public Holidays

Restaurants, shops and tourist sights stay open during most holidays, but may close over the three-day Lunar New Year and Chuseok (harvest festival) holidays.

New Year's Day
1 January

Lunar New Year 18 February 2016, 28 January 2017, 16 February 2018

Independence Movement Day 1 March

Children's Day 5 May

Buddha's Birthday 14 May 2016, 3 May 2017, 22 May 2018

Memorial Day 6 June

Constitution Day 17 July

Liberation Day 15 August

Chuseok 15 September 2016, 4 October 2017, 24 September 2018

National Foundation Day 3 October

Christmas Day 25 December

Safe Travel

Seoul is a safe city, except when it comes to traffic. Drivers tend to be impatient; many routinely go through red lights. For those on foot, don't be the first or last person to cross over any pedestrian crossing and don't expect any vehicles to stop for you. Watch out for motorcyclists, who routinely speed along pavements and across pedestrian crossings.

Telephone Services

Mobile Phones

Korea uses the CDMA network system, which few other countries use, so you may have to rent a mobile (cell) phone while you're in Seoul – though unlocked phones will work fine with local SIMs. Mobile-phone hire and SIM cards are available from KT Olleh, SK Telecom and LGU+, all of which have counters at Incheon International Airport and branches throughout the city.

Phone Codes

Incheon city and airport code ☏032

International access code ☏001

Seoul code ☏02. Do not dial the zero if calling from outside Korea.

South Korea country code ☏82

Mobile phone Korean numbers have three-digit area codes, always beginning with ☏01.

Tourist phone number ☏1330

Toilets

There are plenty of clean, modern and well-signed *hwajangsil* (public toilets). Toilet paper is usually outside the cubicles, but it's wise to carry a stash of toilet tissue around with you just in case. There are still a few Asian-style squat toilets around.

Tourist Information

If you need interpretation help on practically any topic, any time of the day or night, you can call ☏1330.

There are scores of tourist information booths around the city. In major tourist areas look for red-jacketed city tourist guides, who can also help with information in various languages. Handy tourist information centres:

Cheong-gye-cheon Tourist Information Centre (Map p32; Sejong-daero, Gwanghwamun; ◷9am-6pm; ⓢLine 5 to Gwanghwamun, Exit 5)

Dos & Don'ts

➡ Do take your shoes off at any residence, temple, guesthouse or Korean-style restaurant; leave your shoes at the door.

➡ Do give and receive any object using both hands – especially name cards, money and gifts.

➡ Avoid situations that will lead to 'loss of face'.

➡ Don't leave your chopsticks or spoon sticking up from your rice bowl. This is taboo, and only done with food that is offered to deceased ancestors.

➡ Don't blow your nose at the table.

➡ Don't touch food with your fingers, except when handling *ssam* (sesame leaves) for Korean barbecue.

Gangnam Tourist Information Centre (Map p102; http://tour.gangnam.go.kr; 161 Apgujeong-ro, Gangnam-gu; ☺10am-7pm; Ⓢ Line 3 to Apgujeong, Exit 6)

KTO Tourist Information Centre (Map p32; ☎02-1330; www.visitkorea.or.kr; Cheonggyecheon-ro, Jung-gu; ☺9am-8pm; Ⓢ Line 1 to Jonggak, Exit 5)

Insa-dong Tourist Information Centre (Map p32; ☎02-734 0222; Insa-dong 11-gil; ☺10am-10pm; Ⓢ Line 3 to Anguk, Exit 6)

Myeong-dong Tourist Information Center (Map p52; ☎02-778 0333; http://blog.naver.com/mdtic1129; 66 Eulji-ro, Jung-gu; ☺9am-8pm; Ⓢ Line 2 to Euljiro 1-ga, Exit 6)

Travellers with Disabilities

Seoul is slowly getting better at catering for people with disabilities. Many subway stations now have stair lifts and elevators, and toilets for disabled people have been built. A few hotels have specially adapted rooms.

Visas

With a confirmed onward ticket, visitors from the USA, nearly all Western European countries, New Zealand, Australia and around 30 other countries receive 90-day permits on arrival. Visitors from a handful of countries receive 60- or 30-day permits, while Canadians get 180 days.

Language

Basics

Hello.
안녕하세요. *an·nyŏng ha·se·yo*

Goodbye. 안녕히 *an·nyŏng·hi*
(when leaving/ 계세요/ *kye·se·yo/*
staying) 가세요. *ka·se·yo*

Yes./No.
네./아니요. *né/a·ni·yo*

Excuse me.
실례합니다. *shil·lé ham·ni·da*

Sorry.
죄송합니다. *choé·song ham·ni·da*

Thank you.
고맙습니다./ *ko·map·sŭm·ni·da/*
감사합니다. *kam·sa·ham·ni·da*

How are you?
안녕하세요? *an·nyŏng ha·se·yo*

Fine, thanks. And you?
네. 안녕하세요? *ne an·nyŏng ha·se·yo*

What is your name?
성함을 여쭤 *sŏng·ha·mŭl yŏ·tchŏ·*
봐도 될까요? *bwa·do doélk·ka·yo*

My name is ...
제 이름은 *che i·rŭ·mŭn*
. 입니다. *... im·ni·da*

Do you speak English?
영어 하실 줄 *yŏng·ŏ ha·shil·jul*
아시나요? *a·shi·na·yo*

I don't understand.
못 알아 *mot a·ra·*
들었어요. *dŭ·rŏss·ŏ·yo*

Eating & Drinking

Can we see the menu?
메뉴 볼 수 *me·nyu bol·su*
있나요? *in·na·yo*

What would you recommend?
추천 *ch'u·ch'ŏn*
해 주시겠어요? *hae·ju·shi·gess·ŏ·yo*

Do you have any vegetarian dishes?
채식주의 음식 *ch'ae·shik·chu·i*
ŭm·shik
있나요? *in·na·yo*

I'd like ..., please.
... 주세요. *... ju·se·yo*

Cheers!
건배! *kŏn·bae*

That was delicious!
맛있었어요! *ma·shiss·ŏss·ŏ·yo*

Please bring the bill.
계산서 가져다 *kye·san·sŏ ka·jŏ·da*
주세요. *ju·se·yo*

Emergencies

Help!
도와주세요! *to·wa·ju·se·yo*

Go away!
저리 가세요! *chŏ·ri ka·se·yo*

Call ...!
... 불러주세요! *... pul·lŏ·ju·se·yo*

  a doctor 의사 *ŭi·sa*

  the police 경찰 *kyŏng·ch'al*

I'm lost.
길을 잃었어요. *ki·rŭl i·rŏss·ŏ·yo*

I'm sick.
전 아파요. *chŏn a·p'a·yo*

Where's the toilet?
화장실이   *hwa·jang·shi·ri*
어디예요?   *ŏ·di·ye·yo*

It hurts here.
여기가 아파요.   *yŏ·gi·ga a·p'a·yo*

I'm allergic to ...
전 ...에   *chŏn ...é*
알레르기가 있어요   *al·le·rŭ·gi·ga iss·ŏ·yo*

Days & Numbers

yesterday	어제	*ŏ·jé*
today	오늘	*o·nŭl*
tomorrow	내일	*nae·il*
1	하나/일	*ha·na/il*
2	둘/이	*tul/i*
3	셋/삼	*set/sam*
4	넷/사	*net/sa*
5	다섯/오	*ta·sŏt/o*
6	여섯/육	*yŏ·sŏt/yuk*
7	일곱/칠	*il·gop/ch'il*
8	여덟/팔	*yŏ·dŏl/p'al*
9	아홉/구	*a·hop/ku*
10	열/십	*yŏl/ship*

Shopping & Services

I'm just looking.
그냥 구경   *kŭ·nyang ku·gyŏng*
할게요.   *halk·ke·yo*

How much is it?
얼마예요?   *ŏl·ma·ye·yo*

Can you write down the price?
가격을 써   *ka·gyŏ·gŭl ssŏ*
주시겠어요?   *ju·shi·gess·ŏ·yo*

Can I look at it?
보여 주시겠어요?   *po·yŏ ju·shi·gess·ŏ·yo*

Please give me a discount.
깎아 주세요.   *ggak·ka·ju·se·yo*

post office
우체국   *u·ch'e·guk*

tourist office
관광안내소   *kwan·gwang an·nae·so*

Transport

A ... ticket (to Daegu), please.
(대구 가는)   *(tae·gu ka·nŭn)*
... 표 주세요.   *p'yochu·se·yo*

one-way	편도	*p'yŏn·do*
return	왕복	*wang·bok*

Which ... goes to (Myeongdong)?
어느 ...이/가   *ŏ·nŭ ...·i/·ga*
(명동)에   *(myŏng·dong)·é*
가나요?   *ka·na·yo*

bus	버스	*bŏ·sŭ*
metro line	지하철	*chi·ha·ch'ŏl*
	노선	*no·sŏn*
train	기차	*ki·ch'a*

When's the ... (bus)?
... (버스) 언제   *... (bŏ·sŭ) ŏn·jé*
있나요?   *in·na·yo*

first	첫	*ch'ŏt*
last	마지막	*ma·ji·mak*

Accommodation

Do you have a ... room?
... 룸 있나요?   *... rum in·na·yo*

single	싱글	*shing·gŭl*
double	더블	*tŏ·bŭl*

How much per ...?
...에 얼마예요?   *...·é ŏl·ma·ye·yo*

night	하룻밤	*ha·rup·pam*
person	한 명	*han·myŏng*

Behind the Scenes

Send Us Your Feedback

We love to hear from travellers – your comments help make our books better. We read every word, and we guarantee that your feedback goes straight to the authors. Visit **lonelyplanet.com/contact** to submit your updates and suggestions.

Note: We may edit, reproduce and incorporate your comments in Lonely Planet products such as guidebooks, websites and digital products, so let us know if you don't want your comments reproduced or your name acknowledged. For a copy of our privacy policy visit lonelyplanet.com/privacy.

Trent's Thanks

Thanks first up to Megan Eaves for giving me the opportunity to work on *Pocket Seoul* – a seriously great gig! As well as to my co-author, Simon Richmond for all the help and tips. Thanks also to Julia Mellor, Daniel Durrance, Shawn Depress, Daniel Lenaghan and the team from Visit Seoul for their invaluable assistance. A special shout out to all the good folk I met along the road and shared a beer with. But as always my biggest thanks goes to my beautiful girlfriend, Kate, and my family and friends who I all miss back home in Melbourne.

Acknowledgments

Cover photograph: Cheong-gye-cheon, Jack Malipan Travel Photography/Alamy

Image pp4-5: Gyeongbokgung (Palace of Shining Happiness), ontopoint/Getty

This Book

This 1st edition of Lonely Planet's *Pocket Seoul* was coordinated by Trent Holden and researched and written by Trent and Simon Richmond. This guidebook was produced by the following:

Destination Editor Megan Eaves **Product Editors** Kate Chapman, Katie O'Connell **Senior Cartographer** Corey Hutchison **Book Designer** Wibowo Rusli **Coordinating Editor** Simon Williamson **Assisting Editors** Kate Evans, Susan Paterson, Tracy Whitmey, Amanda Williamson **Cover**

Researcher Naomi Parker **Thanks to** Ryan Evans, Andi Jones, Campbell McKenzie, Wayne Murphy, Karyn Noble, Martine Power, Simon Richmond, Samantha Russell-Tulip, Diana Saengkham, Dianne Schallmeiner, Vicky Smith, Lyahna Spencer, Lauren Wellicome, Tony Wheeler

Index

See also separate subindexes for:

✪ Eating p166
♙ Drinking p167
✪ Entertainment p167
⊙ Shopping p167

Sights 000
Map Pages **000**